Lightning
As A
'Photographer'

LIGHTNING
AS A
'PHOTOGRAPHER'

REVISITING A FORGOTTEN PHENOMENON OF NATURE

CHIDAMBARAM RAMESH

Published in association with createspace.com – an Amazon Company

Copyright:	© Chidambaram Ramesh 2013
Cover Design:	Robin Ludwig Design Inc., USA

First Published: June 2013

ISBN-13: 978-1481886758

ISBN-10: 1481886754

CONTENTS

ABOUT THE AUTHOR

Chidambaram Ramesh is a freelance researcher. Currently, he is working to re-discover and re-establish many forgotten, scientifically important ideas of ancient/medieval periods by bringing them under the realm of contemporary science. His first book *'The Shroud of Turin: An Imprint of the Soul, Apparition or Quantum Bio-Hologram'* advanced a new scientific theory to explain the causes of the mysterious image on the Holy Turin Shroud.

DEDICATION

This book is dedicated, as a token of gratefulness and respect, to Professors M. Boudin, Andres Poey, Orioli, Madame Blavatsky, Bill Jay and many others who undertook the task of making several scrupulous efforts to collect and record the various occurrences of lightning impressions.

Acknowledgements

I want to thank several people for their guidance and support. Especially, I thank Ms. Sophia, Image Executive, Science Museum Group, London, Prof. Vladimir A. Rakov, University of Florida, Dr. Mary Ann Cooper, Department of Emergency Medicine, University of Illinois, Mr. Ken Langford, Broomfield, Colorado for their prompt and patient replies to my queries. I am greatly indebted to Dr. Steven Lehar, Research Fellow in Ophthalmology, Harvard University for permitting me to make use of his works relating to Fourier Transformations. It must not be inferred however that these scientists endorse all the views expressed in the book.

For courtesies, information and illustrations and/or permission to reproduce them, I am indebted to the following:

Judie Lipsett Standford, the Editor-in-Chief, *Gear Diary*, Keith Harrison, the Editor, *Shropshire Star*, Miguel Hortiguela, Toronto, Ontario, Canada and K. Kabilan, the Editor, *Free Malaysia Today*.

Ms. Abha Iyengar, my editor, suggested major reorganization of chapters which remarkably improved the clarity of presentation. I would also like to thank my friends for their continued encouragement and support for the work. For the cover design, kind acknowledgements go to the Robin Ludwig Design Inc., USA.

DISCLAIMER

This book is intended to bring together the various cases of 'lightning imprints' and to provide a scientific explanation to them. If the explanation offered in the book hurts in any way the religious sentiments of the readers directly or indirectly, I, as the author, apologize to the readers. The reproduction of illustrations or citations does not necessarily mean that the respective authors agree with the ideas contained in this book.

PREFACE

Go back to Nature; compare our abstracts with her facts,
her workings with our conceptions of them.

—*Argyle*

I began to envision a project on the '*holographic nature of mind process*es' in the year 2010. In search of the instances of spontaneous appearance of photograph-like images in nature, I came across a small article, '*Keraunography*: Notes on the photographic effects of lightning as reported in 19th century journals' (first published in *The British Journal of Photography* on 13th July, 1981), written by Bill Jay. It contained more than a dozen of authentic cases of *lightning figures*, that is, picturesque impressions occasionally made by lightning on human skin, trees, surrounding objects etc. It was so curious that my attention was arrested. Then, I got obsessed with '*Keraunography*' and started searching for similar instances, the result of which is the book you are reading now. Many such cases relating to this are so strange, startling and almost incredible that I decided not to alter the language of their original authentic records.

At this point, I would say that the anecdotal accounts borrowed in the book are interesting and that I am keeping an open mind about them. These are not parables, but real and personal experiences narrated in the contemporary journals and books. Because of their connection to experience, they exhibit reliability and wisdom.

In fact, advancements in science are often made as a result of observations made over long periods of time.

But again, a collection of facts will not make a science. Science warrants reasons and explanations. To bring the entire work to a fitting consummation, I have attempted to provide a plausible explanation to the phenomenon.

The object of this work is *two-fold*: to give a popular account of the phenomenon of lightning imprints and at the same time to increase the readers' insight into the curious phenomenon of nature; also to suggest a theory to attest the phenomenon and of the laws which appear to govern its manifestation.

Today, the boundaries of science have extended in such a way that it has become almost impossible for any researcher to follow up and store in his memory the umpteen facts and discoveries. A comprehensive repository of such instances and facts relating to a particular phenomenon may be always of instant help to any researcher interested in the field. In this work, I have tried to bring together almost all the cases of 'lightning imprints' as I could find in the archives. I can assure the readers that the book contains a greater body of information about the curious photographic effects of lightning than any other work on the subject and it will be a convenient guide to those who wish to investigate this amazing phenomenon of nature. This is a thorough study of the subject, written in non-technical language for the layman with a scientific inclination or just curiosity about nature.

I understand that I am writing this book at the risk of being ridiculed or rejected by the unbelievers. But the contents of this book are not my own imagination. They are authentic records vouched by many great people like Madame Blavatsky of Theosophical Society. So trust this book. Understand that what is told here happened exactly as it had been told.

I would like to conclude the preface with the following.

It is said that the whole course of Nature is a mystery. It is beautiful and beneficial too. I have mentioned in my first book, *"The Shroud of Turin: An Imprint of the Soul, Apparition, or Quantum Bio-Hologram"*, that mystery is a necessary form of communication from the Almighty. All mysteries are perhaps mysteries of science, the understanding of which is always beneficial to humankind. Such wonderful operations of Nature are certainly meant for some great purpose. Let us get behind the veil of Nature's mystery and peep into God's workshop!

Write to: c.ramesh@yahoo.com.
Chidambaram Ramesh
Vellore, India.
11th April 2013.

1

INTRODUCTION

The foolish disregard Me, when clad in human semblance ignorant of my supreme nature, the great Lord of beings; empty of hope, empty of deeds, empty of wisdom, senseless, partaking of the deceitful, brutal and demonical nature'—The Bhagavad-Gita, IX, verse 11.

M an is a work of nature and is always submissible to her laws. He should study the nature around him, learn her laws, observe the immutable rules by which nature acts, and apply these discoveries to his benefits. In fact, all the steps taken by man to improve his existence are a long succession of causes and effects which are nothing more than the development of the first impulse given him by nature. On every aspect of the grand and wonderful operation of nature, there is an unmistakable index of the way the universe is created and evolved. This index is as unerring as a mathematical principle. This grand secret of nature can be understood, not by any laboratory experiments, but by a careful tracing of nature's operations and the consequence of such operations. More treasures of knowledge can be extracted from the long-forgotten mine of all our ancestors learned through observation of Nature herself.

As a result, several old concepts have once again become "new options" for contemporary discussion and research. Nonetheless, it has been the experience of past ages that any idea which is intended to overcome long-existing errors is not easily received. When the idea of the earth being spherical in shape was first announced, it encountered vehement opposition from the learned men of the age. The most enlightened thinkers in those days were frightened, and the Church fought it bitterly. They considered it to be a dangerous doctrine, and condemned all those who assented to it as 'unbelievers.' Even after Magellan, in 1521, had sailed around the earth, the fact that the world is spherical was not accepted and it was two hundred years after when the astronomers finally acknowledged the fact.

History is filled with instances in which some single curious phenomenon of nature provoked investigations which led to important results of scientific truth. The theme of the present work relates to one of such curious phenomenon of nature.

The title *"Lightning as a Photographer"*, itself needs a little explanation here. Occasionally, it happens that when men or animals have been struck by lightning, peculiar impressions have been left upon their bodies, which seem to be the exact impression of some adjacent objects, persons, paintings etc in the vicinity of the stroke. The imprint is so accurate, and sometimes, the exact colours of the original object are also imprinted in such a way that it makes any common observer believe it to be a photographic replica. In this way, lightning sometimes turns out to be a very good photographer!

The book, the tile of which may perhaps scare those who fear novelty, is not a work of imagination; but a collection of facts and experiences. The existence of such lightning imprints may appear, from a theoretical point of view, highly improbable, as the essential conditions of forming a photographic image are wanting. Still, several apparently well-authenticated instances have been recorded, which have led scientific authorities to give at least partial credence to them (*W. & R. Chambers*, 1868).

Cases of this kind are so numerous that M. Boudin, the Chief
Medical Officer of the Military Hospital, du Roule and a researcher,
in his *Treatise on Medical Geography1*, proposed the new term
"keraunography" (in Greek, *Kerauno*—thunder, *graphy*—to
write,) i.e., 'to write with thunder' to catalogue these extraordinary
figures caused by lightning, based on the sincere hope that it will
get its due treatment as a separate branch of science.

Prof. Andres Poey, Director of the *Physico-meteorological
Observatory* at Havana, Cuba, mentioned twenty-four cases of
impressions like photographs made by lightning on the bodies of
men and animals and his little treatise on the subject was published
in 1861 (Paris: Leiber). Of these, eight were impressions of trees
or parts of trees; one of a bird, and one of a cow; four of Crosses;
three of circles or impressions of coins carried about the person;
two of horseshoes; one of a nail; one of a metal comb2; one of a
number of numeral; one of the words of a sentence; one of the back
of an arm-chair.

The phenomenon even came to the attention of Charles Fort, the
famous American writer and researcher. He talks of a 'flap' of
appearances of crosses, "and then other figures" printed upon
windows "in some unaccountable way" in several towns in
Germany in 1872. This was just after the Franco-Prussian War
and some of the images were deemed politically objectionable, so
troopers were sent in to smash them all. Fort then adds: "I have a
collection of stories of pictures appearing on window glass from

---

1   The official title of the book is *"Treatise on the Medical Geography and
     Statistics of Endemic Diseases; Comprising Medical Meteorology and
     Geology, the Statistical Laws regulating population and Mortality, the
     Geographical Distribution of Diseases, and the Comparative Pathology
     of the Races of Man"*

2   A correspondent of Prof. Poey told him that he had known a Trinidad
     lady who had been struck by lightning in her youth and on whose
     stomach the lightning had imprinted a metallic comb which she carried
     in her apron.

American newspapers between 1872 and 1890." Even today, photographs said to be of faces imprinted on windows by lightning are published from time to time in the popular media. (*Fort*, 2004).

Emanuel Santini, editor of the popular scientific magazine *Science en famille*, reported on this occurrence in his text *La photographie a' travers les corps oaques*. Santini contend that the 'lightning writings' were not induced by natural light, but rather by physical radiation. As further causes of photographic recordings, Santini cited electricity, cathode radiation, as well as the then recently discovered X-ray radiation (*Jacques Khalip*, 2011).

Thus, in the annals of Natural history, there are numerous cases of similar experiences. These are attributed not to some supernatural causes but to natural phenomena. The observers who made first-hand records of the phenomenon must not have been scientific experts but could not have confirmed the cases without proper inquiry as to whether the imprints made by lightning were 'photograph-like representations' or merely what the skeptics call *'pareidolia'*—reading something meaningful into an apparently random pattern. Moreover, these observations assume importance especially in a field of study like one relating to lightning, where most experiments just cannot be carried out in a laboratory. These facts cannot be passed off as superstitious beliefs but should rather be evaluated in the light of contemporary scientific developments and knowledge. This is the essence of the whole thing—keep an open mind!

As regards the general scheme of the book, a general introduction as well as some background information is given in this chapter. Some of the curious effects of lightning, gleaned from the annals of the past, are recounted in Chapter 2. This chapter will kindle the interest of the reader towards acquiring a deeper understanding of the nature of lightning. Chapter 3 is the core of the book. In it, many authentically reported cases where the form of some animal or of the human face is clearly and unmistakably portrayed by the act of lightning have been discussed. The cases are so numerous and so authentic that upon completion of this chapter, the reader will have little doubt over the phenomenon of lightning imprints. He may even wonder how this wonderful phenomenon of nature escaped the attention of the researchers.

Chapter 4 discusses how misinterpretation of facts and observations has led to incorrect conclusions about lightning imprints. Chapter 5 contains some curious cases of 'stigmata'—the spontaneous appearance of images and letters on the skin. Their importance for the present book lies mainly in their demonstration of the body's malleability and susceptibility to imprints of images on skin. Chapter 6 attempts to explain the holographic nature of body and the universe and about the Fourier Transforms as a mathematical way of transforming any pattern or design into wave-form and converting the wave-form into respective patterns or images again. It discusses the science of the phenomenon of lightning imprints. Chapter 7 is the concluding part of the book. It advocates that the extraordinary effect of lightning should be viewed in a different light, and should be opened to further investigation by current science.

The very existence of the world depends on the 'laws of nature.' Water, for example, is formed according to the law of nature. Scientists may call it a chemical combination of Oxygen and Hydrogen; but what impelled them to combine? What will happen if the chemical affinity between Oxygen and Hydrogen is suddenly withdrawn? Thus, in the laws of nature, we could find the implicit expression of Divine volitions. In order to understand Divinity, one needs to understand the laws of nature first.

As Daniel Boorstin once said, the greatest obstacle to discovery is not ignorance, but the illusion of knowledge. That is why the discoverer should be always a child at mind. Sit down before fact like a little child, and be prepared to give up every preconceived notion, follow humbly whatever and to whatever abyss Nature leads, or you shall learn nothing!

2

SOME CURIOUS FREAKS OF LIGHTNING

'If there be one time more than another in which man feels that he is entirely in the hands of One mightier than himself, in which all his personal pride sinks in the conviction of his utter helplessness, it is when the forked bolts of heaven glare about him with frightful brightness, and the dread artillery of the skies stuns him with its deafening peals, and shakes the very earth on which he treads'—David Munson

Nature has always played marvelous tricks on humankind. These acts of nature are exceedingly curious. One can hardly examine the records of lightning without being impressed by its freakish actions.

The selectivity of lightning is incredible. Sometimes it undresses its victims, destroys their clothes and leaves the body unhurt. Sometimes, on the contrary, it burns the body and leaves the clothes untouched. In one and the same case, lightning killed the horseman and his horse remained intact, and the other rider remained alive while his horse was burnt to ashes. Keys, watches etc. have been damaged while the persons wearing them are almost uninjured.

Once it tore away the cloth of a sailor's cap at Newport, leaving the lining untouched on his head, and carried off the front of his clothing, while leaving his back covered. The freakish pranks of lightning are well known—the reasons for some of them can be comprehended, but there are many actions of lightning that remain a mystery.

There are other examples. A Negro struck by lightning found, after he had recovered consciousness, that one arm had turned partly white, while the rest of his body remained as black as usual.

A man in Russia ended up in hospital when lightning struck him in the mouth shortly after he took a puff on his cigarette. It went through his body from head to toe. The man's heart stopped beating after the strike and he had apparent death. He remained unconscious for about 24 hours in hospital and then recovered consciousness. (*Lightning strikes man in his mouth for smoking*, 2005).

Dr. Nelson Hendler, clinical director of the Mensana Pain Clinic in Stevenson, Maryland says that one of his patients became an infantile person when he survived a lightning strike. The man started behaving like a two-year old baby.

The Strange Game

In certain cases, lightning plays a strange game, making what seems to be a fastidious choice of its victims. It kills one, spares another, strikes the third, and does good to the fourth!

Madame la Comtesse of the Dechy of Posen wrote to the Flammarion Camille, the French astronomer and author of the renowned book *'Thunder and Lightning'* the following narrative.

"During a storm which took place in the month of August 1901, lightning entered by a half-open door into a stable where there were twenty cows, and killed them. Beginning with that which was nearest the door, the second was spared, the third killed, the fourth

was uninjured and so on. All the uneven numbers were killed, the others were not even burnt."
(*Camille*, 1905).

M. Elisec Duval of Criquetot l'Esneval (Seine-Inferieure) related a very remarkable case. On June 20, 1892, lightning fell on the telegraph poles of Havre and E'tretat. A dozen were thrown over, and the curious part is that every second one was knocked down. (*Camille*, 1905).

Another case of equal interest is here. On February 16, 1866, a thunderstorm descended upon a farm in the commune of *Chapelle Largeau* (Deux-Serves). After a tremendous thunder clap, a young man who was standing near the farm saw an immense fireball touch the ground at his feet, but it did him no damage. It passed, still harmlessly, through a room in the farmhouse in which there were nine persons. The only effect it produced was the flaring up of some matches upon the chimney-piece. It proceeded towards the stables, which were divided into two compartments. In one there were two cows and two oxen; the first cow, to the right of the entrance, was killed, the second was uninjured; the first ox was killed, the second was uninjured. The same effect was found to have been produced in the other compartment, in which there were four cows: the first and the third were killed, the second and fourth were spared; the odd numbers taken and the even numbers left. (*Camille*, 1905).

A similar freak of lightning was reported in the New South Wales papers. A violent storm passed over Terembone, Cartlereagh River, and the lightning which was very vivid, struck a number of cattle in a stockyard knocking the horns off seven, striking one dead and many blind. The remarkable thing is that *only one horn* was knocked off each beast.

In another case, lightning burst open a cupboard, throwing the door away, and damaging the crockery in the most systematic fashion; it broke the first plate, left the second intact, cracked the next, spared the fourth, and so on to the bottom of the pile (*Camille*, 1905).

A case of a similar nature was reported to *'Nature'* by Dr. Enfield from Jefferson, Iowa, United States in about 1902. A house he visited was struck by lightning so that much damage was done. After the occurrence, a pile of dinner plates, twelve in number was found to have every other plate broken (*Lockyer*, 1902).

A very remarkable case of the kind of fanatic choice lightning makes was reported in Japan in the recent past. Experts still fail to explain the reason behind the terrible tragedy. Pupils of a school went for a walking tour and the teacher accompanying the group told the pupils to hold on to a rope. When lightning struck, it killed every second pupil, exactly half the number. The others remained alive. (*Gousseva, Maria*, 2006).

These are few of the most mysterious effects of lightning. However, every action of nature has its own scientific reasons, and the act, when demystified, becomes science. So, for every so-called 'freak of lightning', there should be sound reason.

Though no explanation could be found for the aforesaid phenomenon in the contemporary scientific texts, the following theory was put forth to explain this strange phenomenon as early as in 1816 in the *Encyclopaedia Perthensis*.

"Effects of this kind are generally produced by the most violent kind of lightning called 'ball lightning'—which appear in the form of balls and frequently divide themselves into several parts before they strike. If one of the parts of a fire-ball strikes a man, another will not strike the person who stands immediately close to him. This is because there is always repulsion between the bodies electrified the same way. Now, as these parts into which the balls breaks have all the same kind of electricity, it is evident that they must for that reason repel one another; and this repulsion is so strong that a man may be interposed within the stroke of two of them, without being hurt by either."
(*Brown, 1816*).

The French astronomer Camille Flammarion has cited numerous other cases of the astonishing effects of lightning.

He said, "Lightning has been known to split men in half, almost as with a huge axe. On June 20, 1868, this happened to a miller's assistant at a windmill near Croix. The lightning struck him and split him from his head downward in two."

J.C.M. Boudin of France relates that Captain M. Rihouet of a French frigate *Golymin* was struck by lightning on board his ship on February 21, 1812. On the following day, he could not shave himself; the razor not cutting but tearing out his hair. From that day, the beard disappeared, and the hair of the scalp, eyebrows etc., gradually fell off leaving him entirely bald. The nails of the fingers also scaled away (*Chambers*, 1870).

In a similar instant, *Dr. Gaultier de Claubry* was struck by lightning with the extraordinary result that his beard was taken off from its roots so that it never grew again.

It is an admitted fact that the danger of being struck by lightning is sensibly increased by metals attached to the body of a person. Arago cites a very noteworthy instance of this. On July 21, 1819, lightning fell on the prison of Biberach in Swabia. In the great hall, amidst as many as twenty prisoners, the one struck by lightning was the condemned chief of a band of robbers, who was chained by the waist, while his companions escaped.

During a violent thunder-storm in 1844, a fishing boat near Shetland Islands was struck by lightning. The mast of the boat was torn into slivers. A man who was sitting close by the side of the mast was left unhurt. He was not aware of what had taken place until he found that the watch in his pocket had fused into a mass!

There are many similar allusions to thunder and lightning scattered throughout by the early writers.

Lightning has been known to kill men and animals and leave them standing or lying in perfectly natural positions, but when they are touched, they crumble into dust!

For example, as written in a historical work, the great Con de, coming to a cross-road in the wood of Compiegne, saw a woman standing in the way of his carriage, who did not move aside in spite of his shouts. Becoming impatient at this obstinacy, he gave her a cut with his whip, when the figure immediately fell to dust. It was a mere heap of cinders which had been held together by some miracle. It was learnt that the woman had been struck by lightning a few minutes before.

A curious freak of lightning played on a woman named Ellen Barnes, a laundress, living in the suburbs of Petersburg. She had stepped out to the door and stood holding it, watching the storm, when she was struck by lightning and knocked senseless. Though unable to speak for hours, she was apparently unhurt by the shock. However, due to this, part of her hair had turned a dazzling white!

There is another example of the freakish nature of lightning. During a storm on August 4, 1796, five French soldiers took refuge under a tree and they blamed God for interrupting them in their work. One of them, in the madness of his presumption, took up his firelock and pointing it towards the clouds, said he would fire a bullet at Him who sent the storm! Instantaneously, a flash of lightning struck four of the soldiers dead and wounded the fifth.

The freakish action of lightning sometimes has beneficial effects as well. Once, a powerful stroke instantaneously gouged out a well site, which would have taken many man-hours to dig.

Then there is the instance of the thunder-struck potatoes. Lightning struck a field of potatoes and burned the stalks to cinders, but the potatoes underneath were baked to a turn just as if they had been cooked beneath hot ashes! (*Lane*, 1986).

Lightning appears to have therapeutic effects too. Dr. A. Allison, M.D., Senior Surgeon to the Lloyd Cottage Hospital, Bridlington, reported to the *Lancet* a remarkable case of lightning having therapeutic value, where it helped in curing a malignant tumor. The letter published in the *Lancet* on January 10, 1880, is reproduced below:

"About thirty years ago, I attended Reuben S., a farm labourer, residing at Langtoft, on the Yorkshire Wolds, who suffered from cancer of the inferior lip and part of the chin for about a year, and who had agreed to an operation for their removal. In the meantime he undertook to assist poor farmer for a day in ploughing his land. During this occupation he was struck down by lightning and carried home in a state of insensibility. Both of his horses were killed, and the wooden beam of the plough was split and reduced to considerable fragments. Soon after the occurrence I visited, and found the ploughman in a state of great prostration and emitting a strong odour of ozone, indicating electrical condensation of the adherent oxygen. As soon as reaction took place I bled him from the arm, which act constituted the whole of the treatment. What seems to be the most astonishing feature in the case is the healing process which was set up in the lip and chin soon after the incident. The cancer gradually lessened, and in a few weeks every trace of the diseased structure disappeared, and for ten years he enjoyed complete freedom from his former suffering and signs of the disease. In proof of the specific and hereditary character of the disorder, I may state that the patient's granddaughter Mrs. P. of Driffield, lately became the subject of a cancerous tumour over the larynx, which growth, assisted by Dr. Rames, I removed successfully a few weeks ago, and under the persistent use of arsenical treatment the cure seems to be satisfactory. In S_'s case the electrical fluid seemed to form and pass through two small holes in the head-band of his trousers, and to make its exit by corresponding apertures. After this remarkable exemption from all cancerous development for so long a period, the disease reappeared, and after a year of intense suffering proved fatal; still leaving the inference unaffected that the imponderable element secured from the patient an extension of life, and ten years' relief from the distressing consequence of carcinoma, which circumstance establishes my faith in the therapeutic power of electricity in scirrhous indurations. From the foregoing representation, it is evident that frictional electricity may in good hands become one of the most powerful therapeutic agents in the dispersion of cancerous formations. When cellular hypertrophy takes place in localities favourable to the development of epithelial disease, frictional electricity might be employed for the purpose of destroying the morbid cells, whether in their incipient or advanced stage of progression. The authorities of the London Cancer Hospital will be unfaithful to their honourable trust should they decline to test to the fullest extent the curative effects of frictional electricity in some of the most hopeless variety of diseases to which humanity is exposed. I shall not venture upon any theory of the specific action of electricity on morbid depositions but consign the whole question to the abler readers of your incomparable journal."

Another therapeutic effect of lightning is reported here. In September 1898, at Remains, near Ramerupt (Aube), one Mr. M. Finot, an innkeeper, was standing on his doorstep looking out at a storm, when a flash of lightning followed by a thunderclap sent him flying back into the hall. He remained unconscious for a time, and his sight was affected for ten hours. The extraordinary thing, however, in this case, was that he had been a victim of rheumatism until then, and walked with difficulty and only with the help of a stick, and that ever since this occurrence he had been able to do without the stick, and to pursue his avocations quite comfortably. He felt that he had no reason to regret his experience, though he was not anxious to go through anything of the kind again!

Such examples, of medical treatment made possible by the wonderful effect of lightning, are so numerous that the French astronomer Camille Flammarion suggested that these cases should be treated under a separate title "*Medical Lightning.*"

What follows are more extraordinary cases of where lightning distinguishes between colours, and shows a preference among them.

The 'Black' Prejudice

A report titled, *'Bolt from a Cloudless Sky that Killed Black Sheep only'*, published in the Record-Union (1898), recounts the following instance.

"A thunder storm had passed over the locality just before noon, and the clouds had nearly all broken away or rolled off to the southward. The sun had come out and all uneasiness over the storm had passed when a terrific thunderclap, so close to the earth that it trembled as of from an earthquake, broke from the cloudless noonday sky.

William Arndt had a flock of forty sheep in a pasture a short distance from his farm-house and they had huddled together under a big maple tree in the field while the rain was falling. They were still there when the great thunderclap broke the stillness succeeding the storm. Eighteen of the sheep were black. He found that every one of them had been killed by the strange lightning, while not one of the other sheep were injured. Each dead sheep had a round hole in the back of its neck, around which the wool was burned away."

In another instance at Laplaue in Correze, thunder fell on a grange full of hay and straw, and covered with thatch, without setting it on fire. Then it went to the sheepfold and killed seven black sheep and left the white one.

The 'Red' Favouritism

William Green, in his letter dated 28th September 1774, described yet another remarkable and peculiar effect of lightning.

In the evening of Sunday, the 28th August 1774, there was an appearance of a thunder storm. A gentleman, who was riding near the marshes not far from the town, saw two strong flashes of lightning, seemingly running along the ground of the marsh, at about 9 o'clock in the evening. On Monday morning, when the servants of Mr. Rogers, a farmer at Swanborough in the Parish of Iford, went to the marsh to fetch the oxen to their work, they found one of them, a four-year old steer, standing up, much burnt and scarcely able to walk. By the description of it, it seemed to have been struck with lightning in a very uncommon manner.

The ox was of a red and white colour; the white in large marks, beginning at the rump-bone, and running in various directions, along both the sides; the belly was all white, and the whole head and horns were white likewise. The lightning, with which it must have been undoubtedly struck, fell on the rump-bone, which was white, and distributed itself along the sides in such a manner as to take off all the white hair from the white marks as low as the bottom of the ribs, but so as to leave a line of white hair, about half an inch broad, all around, where it joined to the red. The lightning did not touch a single hair of the red.

Mr. James Lambert at Swanborough, in his letter dated September 13, 1774, mentioned a similar effect of lightning on a bullock in the neighbourhood. The bullock was pied, white and red. The lightning stripped off all the white hair from his back, but left the red hair without the least injury.

In another case reported by Camille Flammarion, lightning struck a young four-year old ox which was red, with white spots. It burnt and removed all the white spots and left the red hair (*Camille*, 1905).

The Mystery of Crop Circles Revealed

Recently, it has been discovered that the microwave emission of lightning make amazing designs in crop fields. These are called 'crop circles'—the geometric patterns that appear mysteriously in crop fields. The crop is not cut but is usually laid flat and most often swirled into an attractive floor pattern. Most patterns appear in crop fields such as wheat, barley, maize, or rapeseed. Crop circles are also referred to as 'Crop Formations' because they are not always circular in shape.

A group of researchers in Russia have claimed that they have solved the mystery of crop circles. According to them, plants bend as a result of microwave emissions caused by lightning strikes. The Russian researcher Anatoly Arzyayev of the All-Russian Electrical Hardware Institute said that the emissions are most likely a result of lightning strikes. He said that they got crop circles at a lawn in their institute 50 years ago when such research was unheard of.

"Two young workers and I were testing high-voltage hardware. The cable that we used to supply the current was hanging 10 meters above the ground when suddenly it discharged an artificial lightning strike on to the lawn below. And the grass bent in even clockwise circles," the researcher said. He added that they conducted several experiments and got crop circles of about 5 meters in diameter.

Another argument backing up this theory is the fact that real crop circles are often accompanied by so-called Lichtenberg figures—narrow strikes of bent. (*Russian Researchers claim to have solved Mystery of Crop Circles*)

This astonishing claim that lightning emits microwaves which affect plants is corroborated by an observation made in Vernon in Franc in about 1872. A garden planted with gooseberry bushes and cherry trees was struck with lightning five or six years previous. Subsequently, everything died around the hole made by lightning, and year by year the 'death circle' increased. A cherry tree planted there died after some years, and gooseberry bushes which had been re-planted, also died subsequently. The cause of the evil, said *Science Pour Tous*, was evidently the lightning, and somehow its morbid action had persisted.

The interesting facts relating to lightning are so numerous and diverse that no theory has yet succeeded in unifying and explaining them. As Camille Falmmarion wrote a century ago, it would be interesting to make a careful study of the 'habits and customs' of lightning. Perhaps in this way we might succeed one day in determining the mysterious nature of these elusive forces.

3

CURIOUS CASES OF LIGHTNING IMPRINTS

*He fills his hands with lightning and commands it to strike its mark—*Job 36:32

A little girl commuted daily to school by foot. One day the weather was cloudy and with slight rain. Yet the girl made her daily trip to school. As the afternoon progressed, the winds whipped up, along with thunder and lightning. The mother of the little girl felt concerned. Her daughter would be frightened as she walked home from school. She herself feared that the electrical storm might harm her child.

Following the roar of thunder, lightning cut through the sky, like a flaming sword. Full of concern, the mother walked through the route to her child's school. On her way, she saw her little girl walking along, but at each flash of lightning, the child would stop, look up and smile. Another and another flash of lightning followed quickly, but with each one, the little girl stopped, looked up and smiled.

Finally, the mother asked her child, "What are you doing?" The child answered, smiling, "God just keeps taking pictures of me."

This is just a story that someone made up to show the innocence of children. But what if it were real? Is the lightning the photographic ray sent by Nature to make snapshots of persons and the scenery it passes through? Or simply put, "Does lightning have photographic qualities?" Many instances say, yes.

Let us now look at some interesting cases of photograph-like image imprinted by the extraordinary effect of lightning. For the sake of convenience, we will refer to these cases of lightning imprints under two categories—*tree-like* images and *un-tree-like* images.

THE IMPRINT OF TREE-LIKE IMAGES

Statements of impressions of trees made on the human body by lightning are not uncommon. The first, though not the earliest, authentic mention of this extraordinary phenomenon was made by no less eminent an authority than Benjamin Franklin, in 1786. He frequently stated the instance of a man who, when standing opposite a tree that had just struck by a thunderbolt, had on his breast an exact representation of that tree. It was afterwards remarked that a reverse image of the tree was indelibly printed upon the breast of this man.

Cases similar to that reported by Franklin of the image of a tree being impressed upon the body of a person struck with lightning have been more than once observed. In August 1853, a little girl was standing at a window before which was a young maple tree, and a complete image of the tree was found impressed on her body after a flash of lightning.

In 1855, M. Raspail mentioned another instance of a boy having climbed a tree for the purpose of robbing a bird's nest. The tree was struck by lightning and the boy was thrown upon the ground. On his chest, the image of the tree, with the bird and nest on one of its branches, appeared very plainly (*Timbs*, 1858).

Professor Andres Poey, Havana, has published a paper of some length on the subject in the *Annual of Scientific Discovery, 1858.* In a particular case, of a person struck by lightning, at Salem, Massachusetts, it was reported that upon his back there was left an impression of a larch tree. This tree was situated just outside the window at which he was sitting.

Madame Blavatsky, the founder of the *Theosophical Society* and a famous author of ancient wisdom reported the case of a boy killed by a stroke of lightning. Imprinted on his chest was the image of a tree which he had been looking at when the lightning bolt struck.

A Cuban newspaper reported in 1852 that lightning struck a palm-tree in the plantation of St. Vincent. It engraved upon its dry leaves a representation of some pine-trees growing in the neighbourhood at a distance of some 340 yards. The image was so perfect that it appeared more like an engraving.

Photographic News for Amateur Photographers (Vol. 3-4) edited by George Wharton Simpson and Sir William Crookes, carries the following anecdote entitled '*Photographic Power of Lightning*':

"We learn from the *Spartansburg Gazette* that at the Gaffney Race Course, near Limestone, shortly after a race, some discussion was going on of the preliminaries of another race at a future day, and many were participating in it around a tree. At this time the sun was serenely setting with no indication of a storm. Suddenly a discharge, loud as a cannon's roar, was heard. The tree was riven by the bolt; and William, a son of Dr. William Nott, leaning against the trunk, was prostrated, as were also some six or eight others, while some four or five were stunned by the electric discharge. Nott lived a few moments only; a man named Long was supposed to be dead, but though frightfully burnt on various portions of his person, and his boots burst by the subtle fluid, he recovered. Mr. Wilwood was also burnt and scarred; Thomas Gaffney was severely shaken; others, to the number of six or eight, were affected. It may not be peculiar to these cases, but those receiving the charge of electricity, when consciousness returned, thought they had been shot, and looked to see whence the balls came, no one thinking of lightning. We have often heard of the photographic power of electricity, but this is the only instance in which this phenomenon has been certified to us. It was on the person of young Nott. On the front surface of the thigh was indelibly impressed the perfect branch of a tree, leaves and all; and this notwithstanding the part was protected by his pantaloons and drawers. The figure was distinct in all its parts, and of a reddish purple hue."

There are several other instances of such impressions. For example, in a magazine called '*Society*' in 1903, the following was stated.

During a shooting competition at Pont, in the Canton Vaud, the grand stand was struck by lightning, and 25 persons received shocks from which, however, they sustained but little physical injury. One most singular effect however remained. Every person who had felt the electric shock had, photographically stamped either upon the back, the face, or the arms, the reflection of the pine trees behind the firing line. (*Society*, 1903)

The American Photographer, in its October 1774 issue, carried the following story:

A phenomenon occurred at Ellenville during a thunderstorm. A youth of about 17 years sat near the window during the storm and despite the warning voice of his mother, who spoke to him of the lightning rods placed just outside of the window, he insisted on remaining, saying he was not afraid. Scarcely had he spoken, when a sudden flash prostrated him, rendering him insensible. On opening his shirt front to give him air, people were startled to perceive the likeness of an adjacent old apple tree plainly pictured in lines on fire on his breast. It remained distinctly visible for several hours. Fortunately, beyond rendering the young man insensible and giving him a sickening sensation, the effect of the lightning wore off after a short time. (*Our Views*, 1884).

Here is another strange example. On one Monday in the year 1831, about noon, the village of Horsforth was visited by a tremendous thunder-storm. The house of George Lawson was struck by the electric fluid; a square of glass was broken and the plastering above the window cracked; in the window were seven plants in pots, and each pot was placed in a white saucer; the electric fluid drove the saucers from under two of the pots, leaving them in their original situation, and struck three of the children, all of whom were knocked down and remained extremely sick for some time after. It is remarkable that the eldest child aged 11 years was burnt upon her left arm by the lightning and an impression exactly corresponding with the branch of the *Aloysia citro-odora*, one of the plants from under which the saucer had been driven, made upon it. Another little girl, aged three years, was burnt upon the thigh precisely in the same manner, and upon the left arm, with a representation of the flower of the same plant; and the little boy of six years of age was slightly burnt upon his foot; the other members of the family escaped unhurt. (*Murray*, 1833).

Another example of a body imprint by lightning occurred in Americus, Georgia some time before 1886. A little girl, says the *San Francisco Bulletin*, was playing under a cherry tree when a thunderstorm came up. Following a particularly vivid flash of lightning the child fell and when picked up was found to have a perfect and beautiful representation of a limb of the cherry tree photographed upon her right hip. Every twig and leaf was delicately yet distinctly traced in light red lines. The child recovered and bore the imprint of the branch for at least a month.

Poey reported a personal example, in his '*Memoir on Lightning Storms in Cuba and the United States*'. On 24 July 1852, a poplar tree in a coffee plantation was struck by lightning. On one of the large dry leaves was found an exact representation of some pine-trees that "lay at the distance of 339 meters (367 yards 9 inches)." (*Timbs*, 1858).

The *Comptes-rendus*, of the Academy of Sciences at Paris, affirm that the image of a poplar leaf was found upon the body of a magistrate and upon that of a miller's boy, who were both struck by lightning at the same time and by the same flash. This occurred in 1841 in a village of the *Departement de IIsere*. *The Cambridge Independent* is the source for the following incident:

"In the year 1862, the hamlet of Aldreth Huddenham was visited by a thunderstorm. In this place there were two cottages standing in a lone spot, occupied by Daniel Cockle and John Stokes, labourers. About five yards from Cockle's house, and in an adjoining field, there is a young elm-tree. The tree was struck by lightning; the fluid travelled from there in a very indirect line to the farther house, entering the back door, which was open. Ann Stokes, aged fourteen years, was standing in this room, not facing the doorway, but near the middle of it and in a line with the door. The electric fluid struck the girl's lower extremities, paralyzing both feet and producing an imprint upon the left leg and thigh, of the colour of scarlet, and in every respect resembling the tree itself, namely, the trunk, the branches, and the leaves, and in the most beautiful model form it is possible to conceive. She has regained the use of her limbs and the daguerreotype appearance is fading away. Strange to say, her dress was not in any way injured by the electric fluid."
(*John Holmes Agnew*, 1862).

A young woman, in 1872, while standing behind a window at Morgantown, Butler County, Kentucky, received a slight shock from a flash of lightning. It was found that an *ailanthus* tree standing near the window had been identifiably and accurately photographed upon her breast by the electric flash.

A concluding instance of the body being imprinted by lightning occurred at Whalley Range, near Manchester, England, in 1866. Three boys had gone out for a walk in the Range. Their names were Edwards, Greenhough, and Jones, the first two residing on Cedar Street and the latter on Erskine Street, in Manchester. Overtaken by a severe storm, they took refuge under a tree with large, over-spreading branches. They had not been long in this shelter when a vivid flash of lightning circled the tree in a curiously serpentine fashion. All the boys were partly stunned by the shock. Edwards, who was the most seriously affected, presented on his left side the perfect image of a tree, the trunk, leaves, and branches of which were outlined with photographic accuracy. The impression of the tree was reproduced less distinctly on the boy's right side, but both pictures graduated from the knee, terminating and joining at the apex of the chest.

Similar cases of tree-like imprints made by lightning are so numerous that I need not give further instances. There is another reason for limiting the cases relating to imprint of tree-like images and a detailed discussion of the topic must await the next chapter. Now, we shall learn about and be amazed at the imprint of *un-tree like* images on the body by lightning.

THE IMPRINT OF UN-TREE-LIKE IMAGES

Crosses Imprinted on Human Bodies:

The first mention that appears to have been made of lightning-imprints is found in a work of one of the so-called Fathers of the Church, St. Gregory of Nazianz. He affirmed that in the year 360 A.D., images were printed by lightning upon the bodies and clothes of the workmen occupied in rebuilding the temple of Jerusalem.

The Jews had been called upon by the Emperor Julian to reconstruct their temple. The labourers were occupied with the foundation-work, when an earthquake took place. It was preceded by a whirlwind and tempest, which suddenly arose and forced them to take shelter in a neighbouring church. According to St. Gregory—a contemporary of the Emperor Julian, and the only one who has left a detailed description of the circumstances—during the tempest, 'globes of fire were seen to proceed from the earth', and the workmen who had taken refuge in the church had certain 'figures of crosses' mysteriously printed upon their clothes and their bodies. These crosses were said to have been dark or invisible during the day but brilliant or phosphorescent in the darkness of night. (*William Chambers*, 1861).

In later periods, similar impressions of crosses upon the body by the action of lightning were noticed by the Rev. Dr. John Still, Bishop of Wells, in Somersetshire, and it was recorded by Isacc Casaubon in his *Adversaria* about the year 1610-1611.

"It appears that one summer day in the year 1595, when the people were attending divine worship in the cathedral of Wells, two or three claps of thunder were heard, which frightened them so much that they all threw themselves upon the ground. Lightning fell without hurting anyone present, but, strange to relate, crosses were found to have been printed upon the bodies of those who attended the church. The bishop's wife made the discovery and informed her husband that she had the figure of a cross imprinted upon her body, which she regarded as the effect of a miracle. The bishop laughed at her, but immediately found a similar mark upon his own body (on his arm). Others had these crosses upon their shoulders, or upon their breasts, and they were witnessed by many persons." (*William Chambers*, 1861)

Joseph Grünpeck (1473-1532), physician and scholar of diverse talents has also mentioned crosses appearing on clothing in his *Speculum naturalis cœlestis* (1508).

Another case of crosses printed probably by lightning is on record: it happened during the eruption of Mt. Vesuvius3 in 1660. The fact was communicated to Father Kircher who published a long dissertation upon it in 1661, entitled *"Diatribes de prodigiogis Crucibus Quoe post ultimatum Incendium Vesuvii Montis Napoli Comparuerunt'*. A copy of this work exists in the *Bibliotheque de Ste Genevieve (Sainte-Geneviève Library)* of Paris. It informs us that after the eruption of the volcano, crosses were seen upon various articles of linen, such as shirt-sleeves, women's aprons, and table-cloths, which were exposed to the open air during the volcanic phenomenon. According to Kircher, 30 such images were found on one altar cloth, and eight on the "flank" of a child. They

---

3   A strato-volcano in the Gulf of Naples in Italy.

varied in colour, size and style; they were difficult to clean off and while most faded, some lasted more than 10 days. This may well be the phenomenon depicted in medieval woodcuts as a "rain of crosses" (*Rickard*).

Picture of Crucification on the Back

Utica Herald Dispatch carried the following story titled 'Image of Christ on Man's Back.'

"On 5th August 1904, in Morristown, New Jersey, a man named Abbott Parker, a wandering painter, while walking along the street, was struck by a bolt and knocked unconscious. Parker was found by Theodore Armstrong and was taken to All Souls' Hospital. When Parker was picked up large streaks were noticed all over his back. On his arrival at the hospital, the streaks on the man's back began to assume the form of a Cross and as the sisters and doctors watched the marvelous transformation, the figure began to grow more distinct and soon the image of Christ nailed to the cross appeared. The nails in His hands and feet were as plain as if they had been painted there. The wound in the side could be seen and upon the head of Christ appeared the Crown of thorns as distinctly as upon the large crucifix which hung directly over the young man's head."
(*Utica Herald Dispatch*, 1904)

In some mysterious manner, the large crucifix which hung directly above the head of the bed upon which Parker was laid was connected with the picture upon his back and it was generally accepted as a partial explanation of the phenomenon, but in fact, it rather deepened the mystery.

The nuns believed that it was a miracle, and the doctors were mystified, as they declared that the picture was not the result of tattooing. A theory which seems generally accepted is that Parker's skin had become sensitized by the effect of lightning, and acted as a photographic plate for the crucifix hanging over his cot. The patient on his recovery said that he was never tattooed. (*A Human Camera—Mystery of a Picture*, 1904). Edward Gravel, an expert tattooer, after examination, also decided that the picture was not tattooed and described it as follows. "The markings on the back of Abbott Parker were not tattooed on him and bear no resemblance to tattoo marks. It is not even possible that the picture was tattooed on the man year ago and has not been restored by the lightning. When the man says that he never was tattooed, he is telling the exact truth. In the first place the coloring of the picture is not at all such as it would be if it had been tattooed on his back and I know of no color tattoers use which would produce such a result I saw." (*The St. Louis Republic*, 1904).

Dr. J.B. Griswold said that he had made as careful an investigation of Parker's case as was possible under the circumstances, and that he had found nothing to indicate deception. "When I first saw Parker," he said, "his back showed a heavy burn, apparently the result of lightning. There was nothing remarkable about the case then, and after doing what I could to relieve the man I went to my other patients. It was about 5 o'clock that I was called and told of the picture of the cross which was then faintly appearing upon his back. Two hours later, I again saw him and there was the picture complete and perfect in its outlines." (*The American Amateur Photographer*, 1904).

Chisholm Herald, in its edition of 2nd December 1904, held that the most severe and exhausting tests were tried by physicians suspecting deception, but they failed to find anything of the kind and were emphatic in declaring the picture could not have been printed on the back by artificial methods.

The New York Times (5th May 1907 edition) bore an advertisement announcing that Abbott Parker, the man with the cross on his back, was the principal feature at Huber's Fourteenth Street Museum for people's view. It therefore appears that the picture on Parker's back had continued to exist years after.

Girlfriend's Image on His Back

An article *"Lightning's Queer Freaks: Seems to make a specialty of Tattooing Images on Victims"* appeared in *"The News and Courier"* July 30, 1908 and *The Pittsburg Press* on August 8, 1908.

A 19-year old youth Joseph Cambon in the Bronx district of New York City was knocked down by a blinding flash of lightning while walking along a shaded street under a row of poplar trees during a thunderstorm. He was picked up, carried to a neighbouring house and soon regained consciousness.

He complained of a severe pain—a burning sensation on his back. When his clothing was removed, it was discovered, to the astonishment of those present, that the outlines of a pretty girl's face had been tattooed on the skin below his shoulder blades by the lightning. The image stood out with startling distinctness in vivid red lines. Stranger still, the girl was easily recognized as a belle of the neighbourhood.

"Why, it's Shade.K!" exclaimed one of the attendants. The young man was completely non-plussed when he heard this, for it was the girl with whom he was keeping company. He then acknowledged that he had a small photograph of the girl pasted on the inside of his watchcase, which he was carrying in his vest pocket.

Chinese Inscriptions on the Arm

The Morning Oregonian, 9th July 1906, carried the following story about an odd freak of lightning.

"Mrs. Thomas Lynch was picking lettuce in her garden at 416, Fulton Street, Union Hill, New Jersey, one afternoon when remarkable storm descended. She went to her gate with a glass dish in her hand. Just then lightning struck so close by that her hand, touching the gate, felt the shock. She found that her fingers clasped the dish so tightly that she could not put it down. After some hours, the feeling of numbness left her arm, her hand lost its cramp, and she could loosen her hold on the dish.

Next morning, the arm became black and swollen. On it, between the shoulder and elbow, pale figures began to appear. Finally, they showed, plainly printed on the skin, a picture of a bird resembling a pheasant, a picture of a snake and characters like the Chinese inscriptions on boxes of tea.

A correspondent of the *New York World* at Union Hill who saw these strange devices on Mrs. Lynch's arm, attested the incident and stated that the marks were of reddish colour and remarkably clear." (*Morning Oregonian*, 1906).

Images of Metal Objects

The following anecdotes are typical of a great mass of others. They tell of metallic objects printed on the skin; of clothes, while being worn, receiving impressions of neighboring objects, or of the skin being pictured with surrounding scenery or objects, during thunder-storms.

On 14th November 1830, lightning struck the Chateau of Benatonnieve, in La Neudie. The next day, one of the inmates remarked upon a peculiar design the back of a lady's dress which happened to be a faithful copy of the ornaments on the back of one of the chairs in a saloon of the Chateau. The lady to whom the dress belonged remembered that she was sitting in that chair at the time of the storm. The image, we are told, was so distinct that it appeared as if it had been recently copied with great pains, from the design at the back of the chair. These facts were related to Dr. Baudin by M. de. Bessay who was present on the occasion. (*Marvellous Freaks of Lightning*, 1916).

M. Jose Maria Dau, of Havana, records that in 1838, in the province of Candaleria in Cuba, there was found on the right ear and on the right side of the neck of a young man struck by lightning the reproduction of a horseshoe, which had been nailed up at a short distance from him against a window. (*Camille*, 1905).

Doctor's Monogram found in Thief's Pocket

A curious story is told of Dr. Derendinger, a Viennese doctor. In the summer of 1865, he was returning home by train. In his pocket was his highly valued tortoise-shell wallet decorated with a large and distinctive silver monogram—two D's intermingled. On getting out at the station, he found that he had not got his purse on him—someone probably had stolen it. Sometime after, the doctor was called to attend to a stranger who had been found lying insensible under a tree having been struck by lightning. The first thing that he noticed on examining the man's body was that on his thigh there was a reproduction as though by photography, of his own monogram. His astonishment may be imagined. He succeeded in reviving the stranger, who was taken to a hospital. The doctor remarked that in his clothes his lost tortoise-shell purse would probably be found. So it proved. The individual struck by lightning was the thief. The electric fluid had been attracted by the steel plate, and had imprinted the monogram upon the man's body. (*Camille*, 1905).

There are also on record instances of women being struck by lightning while holding a pair of scissors and the scissors being clearly imprinted on the chest or arm.

There is another instance of a horse shoe being imprinted on the back of a sailor. In September, 1852, the brigantine Il Buon Servo was anchored in Armiro Bay at the entrance to the Adriatic Sea. Here she was struck by lightning. In obedience to a superstition, the Ionian sailors had attached a horseshoe to the mizzenmast as a charm against evil. When the lightning struck a sailor seated by this mast was instantly killed. There were no marks or bruises upon his person, but the horseshoe was perfectly pictured upon his back.

The Chronicle concluded with the account of a Spanish brigantine which was struck by lightning while in the roads at Zanta. Five sailors were at the prow, three of them awake and two of them sleeping. One of those sleeping was killed and when he was undressed the figures **4.4**, plain and well-formed, were found imprinted on his breast. His comrades swore these figures were not there before his death, and their original was found in the rigging of the vessel. This case was one among the four cases brought before the Scientific Congress at Naples by Professor Olioli, a very learned Italian.

Images of Animals Printed on the Human Body

Image of a Cow

A quite impressive number of these so-called lightning imprints upon the human body have been recorded.

In 1857, *the San Francisco (California) Chronicle* cited several interesting examples. One of these was the case of a country-woman who had arrived in Paris from the Department of Seine et Marne. Many said that her case should be presented to the French Academy of Sciences. This woman had, a short time before, been watching a cow in an open field when a violent storm arose. She, together with the cow, took refuge under a wide-spreading tree which at that instant was struck by lightning. The cow was killed by the bolt and the woman fell to the ground unconscious. When she was found some time later by neighbors and her clothing removed to revive her, the exact image of the cow killed at her side was found impressed upon her breast. (*Splitter*, 1955).

Image of a Black Cat

The human body itself seems subject to such "lightning" impressions. Somewhat ludicrous, but carefully authenticated, is the odd result of a lightning flash in Hilldale County, Michigan, in 1887.

"On a summer evening a tremendous thunderstorm passed over that region, during which the play of lightning was vivid and almost incessant. Just before the storm broke, Amos J. Biggs, a farmer living about midway between Hillsdale and Jonesville, a man who was quite bald with a smooth and shiny pate, went out into his backyard to frighten away some cats who were fighting on the woodpile. He made various feints and gestures, but so intent were they upon their mutual hatred that they allowed him to come within a few feet of them. Just as he was about to cudgel them with a large stick, there came a tremendously bright flash and simultaneously a crash as lightning struck the woodpile, annihilating the cats and scattering blocks of wood in every direction. The fluid passed down Mr. Biggs' body breaking the cover of his watch and neatly extracting his left trouser leg from top to bottom and finally bursting his left boot, tearing the sole cleanly away from the upper. But apart from a prickly sensation and a sudden contraction of the muscles Biggs suffered no unpleasant effects.

When Biggs reentered the house after this experience his wife took one look at him and fainted. Her first words upon recovering consciousness were, "Oh, Amos, the devil has set his mark on you!"

Biggs looked into the mirror and was disconcerted to find the image of a black cat silhouetted on his shiny pate. The cat's whiskers, teeth, even the hair on its tail were reproduced in exquisite, minute detail. Biggs and his wife tried to remove the obnoxious portrait using such homely stain-removers as soap, scouring bricks, vinegar, ashes, all to no purpose. The simple passage of hours effected what scouring blocks could not and by the next morning the picture was much faded. By noon it had disappeared completely."
(*Splitter*, 1955).

Image of a Pug Dog

Western Electrician, 1887, Vol.1 (page 139) carries the following story.

"One of the handsomest and most popular belles of Lincoln, Nebraska, was a few days ago the owner of a little pug dog. During a storm, the dog was frightened by the noise of the elements, and took refuge in the bedchamber of his mistress. She happened to be engaged in changing her dress at the moment, but noticing the extreme agitation of the little pug, she took him in her arms to reassure and comfort him. At that instant a loud dash of rain attracted her attention, and she drew the curtain aside to peep out. Just then came a blinding flash of lightning and the young lady fell to the floor, stunned and unconscious. Other inmates of the house, hearing the fall, came in and found her. The little dog was killed by the shock, and it was hours before the young lady recovered animation. When she did so, she was horrified to find that an image of her dog, life size, had been photographed on her bosom. There seems to be no way of removing the picture which gives every shade, color and wrinkle of the canine form." (*Instances of Photography by Lightning*, 1887).

Imprint of Numerals and Letters

A paper published in the *Journal des Sarants* in 1690, by the Abbe Lamy, puts us in possession of another curious fact relating to lightning-impressions. On July 18, 1689, lightning struck the tower of the Church of St. Sauveur at Langy in France, and in an instant, printed upon the cloth of the altar some *Latin* words of a prayer book. The words *Qui pridie quam pateretur etc* to the end of the prayer, were all reproduced, with the exception of '*Hoc est corpus meum*', and '*hic est sanguis meus*', which were printed in **red ink**, whilst the others were in black characters. The only difference remarked between the two sets of characters—namely those of the prayer-book and those printed by the lightning flash—was that the latter were reversed. (*J.D. Bell*, 1869).

According to Lamy, the curtains surrounding the altar were blown off their rings, but without breaking the rings or detaching them from the curtain-rail or ripping the cloth. Altar cloths were burnt in various places, and the main cloth was torn in a huge X-shaped rent. The incident that aroused the greatest astonishment and terror was the appearance of strange lettering across the main altar cloth. The text of the service card was reversed and magnified but, horror of horrors, the holiest words regarding Christ's flesh and blood—*Hoc est corpus meum*, and*Hic est sanguis meus*—were missing. Father Lamy was a match for this diabolical trick, seeing immediately that the omitted words were those printed in red ink on the card and that the lightning had transmitted only the main part of the text printed in black ink.

A couple of centuries later, Flammarion re-examined the records and concluded that Lamy's report was factual (*Camille*, 1905).

It was assumed at the time, by those persons conventionally scientific of mind, that the altar cloth was damp at the time of exposure, perhaps contained some metallic salts, and since the lightning bolt struck at night, the photographic impression had time to become dry and permanently fixed in the cloth 'plate' before morning. Yet this hardly explains the mystery of the impression being received by the portion of the cloth beside, rather than under or above, it.

There is another account of great marvel, and Professor Orioli was the source of the account. It is as follows.

On October 9, 1836, a young man was found struck by lightning. He was wearing a 'girdle' (presumably a money belt) containing a few gold coins. These coins were imprinted on his skin in the same manner they were placed in the pouch—producing a series of circles on the skin.

Perhaps the most important of all in this case were the facts brought forth in the report of the physician Dicapulo, who attended the unfortunate sailor. He says:

"After undressing the young man we found a band of linen tied about his body in which were gold pieces done up in two paper-wrapped parcels. The parcels on the right side contained a letter from Spain, three guineas, two half-guineas and one smaller piece; the parcel on the right side contained another letter, four guineas, a half-guinea and two smaller pieces. Neither the gold coins, the paper, nor the linen were in the least damaged; but upon the sailor's right shoulder were six distinct circles, appearing as though traced upon his skin. These circles, which all touched at one point, were of three different sizes and exactly correspond with the gold pieces in the right side of his belt." (*Timbs*, 1858).

Flower and Umbrella Imprints

Madame Morosa, an Italian lady of Lugano who, while sitting at her window during a storm in 1847, felt a severe shock and the image of a flower was so indelibly printed upon her leg that she preserved the mark for many years.

In 1900, a gentleman killed by lightning at Harrogate was found to be impressed with a print, 'or lightning photograph' of the umbrella which he was carrying at the time.

CURIOUS CASES OF LIGHTNING IMPRINT ON TREES, ANIMALS, & OTHER OBJECTS

Lightning creates imprints on all kinds of surfaces, even animals, trees and other objects.

Imprint on a Rabbit

The following is a graphic account of lightning's freak effects.

"A rabbit was shot by Jasper Barrett near his Jefferson, South Carolina, home in February 1971. While it was being prepared for supper, his wife and a friend saw the outline in black of a woman's face on the skinned flesh of one foreleg. It was about an inch across with a rosebud mouth, curly hair and long lashes, reminding its viewers of the fashions of the 1920s. Curtis Fuller, reporting the story in *Fate* (October, 1971) noted that within a week of the news appearing in the *Charlotte Observer*, about 4,000 people had trekked to see it, and for several days extra police were deployed to control the crowds.

Another still more extraordinary case occurred in the year 1812. It was related by Mr. James Shaw to the members of the *Meteorological Society of London*. In the year named, there existed near the village of Combe Bay, about four miles from the town of Bath, an extensive wood, composed chiefly of oaks and nut-trees. In the centre of the wood was a pasture-ground of some fifty square yards in extent, where six sheep were killed by the lightning. When the skins of these animals were afterwards taken off, it was observed that the internal portions of each separate skin bore the most faithful image of the surrounding landscape—every details of which was distinctly printed upon the skins.

When the skins were taken from the animals, says Mr. Shaw, 'a *facsimile* of a portion of the surrounding scenery was visible on the inner surface of each skin I may add that the small field and its surrounding wood were so familiar to me and my school-fellows, that when the skins were shown to us, we at once identified the local scenery so wonderfully represented.' These skins were exposed to public gaze for some time, as a curiosity, in the town of Bath.
(*William Chambers*, 1861).

Imprints on Trees

A remarkable phenomenon illustrating photography by lightning was discovered by some workmen in Belfast, Northern Ireland in the year 1908. The men employed by the Ulster Furnishing Company, York Street, were sawing a log of mahogany which was found to contain right through a very clearly-defined 'photograph' of a small deer and a larger animal running. Doubtless the 'photograph' was transmitted by lightning during a storm and the picture must have been 'taken' by long time ago, as the tree, being 4 ft. in diameter, was an exceedingly old one. Every plank of the log right through, we are told, showed the image clearly. (*Photography by Lightning*, 1908).

Trees struck by lightning have sometimes excited much astonishment from letters, figures and other devices being found engraved in the heart-wood, often at a foot from the surface, and as much from the centre. Crucifixes, images of the Virgin, rings and other objects have also been found in the like circumstances.

In the church of the White Nuns of the Order of St. Augustin at Maestricht, is preserved the figure of a Crucifix said to have been found in the heart of a walnut-tree on its being split by lightning.

The Pittsburgh Press, in its January 29, 1922 edition published a statement regarding lightning as a photographer sent in by Candler Cobb, an American Trade Commissioner.

"In the heart of an old beech tree recently cut up on the Island of Skye, there were found burnt marks in the very heart of the tree showing a man's name and the date "10-9-90". It is supposed that these figures were photographed on the interior of the tree by the electrical effect of lightning striking near the spot." (*Google News*)

Hologram Like Photo of a Boat

Among the queer tricks played by flashes of lightning is that of photographing a steam boat on a plate glass mirror. The mirror was sent from Chattanooga, Tenn, to Decatur, Ala by way of a Tennessee River boat, and during the night a heavy thunder shower came up. While the storm was at its height, another steamboat passed the first, and it was observed that the second boat was reflected in this mirror which was on the lower deck of the first boat, facing the water.

No particular attention was paid to the incident until the owner, standing almost parallel with the mirror, happened to glance across its surface. There he saw a perfect photograph of the river craft. It was found upon investigation that the likeness could not be removed, and could be seen only from one angle. (*Lightning as a Photographer*, 1904).

The Photograph on the Wall

The New York Times published an article 'The Queer Photograph on the Wall: Effect of a Vivid Flash of Lightning some years ago', taken from the *Rochester Democrat*.

"During a violent electric storm in early summer a frame house on the west side of west street, in Fairport was struck by lightning, its chimney was struck by lightning, its chimney demolished, and some damage done to the inside of the house. It is also believed that a tree in the yard near the house was struck, but this cannot be accurately stated.

In an upper front room of the house, which was then nearly a new one, was a 'blank white wall', opposite the two windows which faced the street looking eastward. On this blank wall was at once found an exact picture of the outside front of the house just as it appeared from the street. The picture was perfect and distinct as a photograph on a negative. The wonder was visited by scores of persons, including the elder pupils of the Fairport School, and for a few days afforded a topic of conversation but soon it faded." (*The Queer Photograph on the Wall*, 1896).

An Angel in the Picture

"A curious lightning freak occurred during an electrical storm which swept over the village of Rome, Indiana. At an old fashioned tavern, a bolt struck the building, shattering the dining room windows and burned an engraving from its frame, leaving the frame intact, but printing the original design of the picture on the wall paper back of the frame, which was left hanging. (*Chronicling America*, 1911).

A comparable occurrence took place in Mount Olive, North Carolina, late in the year 1890. A photograph of a certain John Taylor—formerly resident in the community but deceased before this event—stood on the mantelpiece of J. H. Smith, merchant in the village, when lightning struck the building. The bolt entered at the chimney head, traversed the mantel and demolished the frame of the Taylor portrait, leaving the picture itself unharmed.

Nevertheless, something strange had happened to the picture. Now there appeared the clearly defined impression of an angel, with outstretched wings overshadowing the deceased Mr. Taylor's head, arms encircling his neck. The right hand of the angel held a nosegay of flowers; the pose suggested protection and benediction. A dark line showing the lightning's journey along the cardboard turned abruptly just above the face of Mr. Taylor, as though the angel had turned aside the course of the electrical fluid.

Some people of the community believed it to indicate that Taylor was safe and blessed in heaven. Mr. Smith, however, declared that the mystery picture of the angel corresponded exactly with an engraving on the back of another photograph standing nearby. By some lightning freak, he believed the picture of this angel had been transferred to the Taylor portrait. This photograph with its angel "protector" was exhibited for some time in J. H. Smith's store in Mount Olive and caused a great deal of comment." (*Splitter*, 1955).

Politicians' Features on a Wall

In the United States of America, an immense barn had been built by a man named Abner Millikan, an ardent republican who adorned the front walls of his farm with portraits of McKinley and

Hobart4. During a violent storm that broke out, the building was struck by lightning several times, and it looked as though it were enveloped in great sheet of flame. Millikan, who had been at some distance from the spot, rushed there much alarmed, and found to his relief that no damage had been done. The portraits alone had been destroyed and—here is the strange detail—the lightning had traced the politicians' features upon the wall.
(*Camille*, 1905).

Letters Embedded on Sugar Candy

During a thunderstorm in Mobile a flash of lightning played one of the strangest tricks ever known. It went into the photographing business without the aid of any apparatus, except an object to be photographed and a piece of sugar candy for a receiving plate.

In the candy store of Mr. Tonsmeire on lower Dauphin Street, was the candy that the lightning chose to operate upon. The candy was of sugar and glucose, brown in color and transparent. It lay on a slab on a table in the midst of the store. The article photographed was the wrapper of small American Flags then lying imbedded in some melted candy on the floor of the store, in front of the table, but not in line of view of the candy on the table. On the wrapper was an inscription in condensed gothic type, reading "National Flags." This inscription, beginning with the fourth letter of the first word and part of the third letter, just so much of the lettering as was visible on the wrapper as it lay in the midst of the stocky stuff on the floor was taken by the lightning and transferred to a piece of the candy on the table; not transferred simply, but imbedded in it, beneath the surface the smallest fraction of an inch. It was a perfect reproduction and perfectly black, but inserted face front, just as in the original, and not reverse, as would be the orders of the letters if

---

[4]   William McKinley and Garret Augustus Hobart were respectively the President and Vice-President of the United States during the 1880s.

anyone should attempt to transfer them by applying the wrapper to the surface of the candy.

In a search for a clue to the sudden and mysterious appearance, the paper wrapper was discovered on the floor with those letters exposed which appeared on the candy. Mr. Fosdick said that there was a mirror in front of the table that possibly had something to do with the photographing.
(*The Saint Paul Globe*, 1897).

Image of a Waste Paper Basket

One of the most interesting acquisition to the Science Museum, South Kensington, is a memento of the great thunderstorm of July 10, 1923 when London was kept awake all night by the reverberations. A flash of lightning printed, in the photographic sense, the image of a wastepaper basket on the bare wooden floor of a city office, and the negative, if it may be so called, reproduced every stare and band in the basket. The section of floor was sawed out and acquired by the Museum. (*Photograph by Lightning*, 1923).

Scenery Pictured on Stones

Mr. Patterson, the editor of the *Qquaqua Spectator*, Illinois, had a stone containing a photographic impress of a beautiful landscape. It was about four inches long by two inches in width; the picture represented, in their true colors, a bluff or bank of yellow clay, the meandering line of a creek lined with willows and cotton woods, and a spring crowned with a large tree. This landscape is the correct representation of a view in the Warren County, Illinois. Mr. Patterson attributed the picture to the action of electricity during a thunder storm, while the image had been reflected on the surface of the stone. (*A petrifaction and natural Dageuerreotype on Stone*, 1856).

Another curious freak of nature was discovered in New Mexico in February, 1890. Colonel A. C. Hawley, formerly Adjutant General of Minnesota, was in possession of a curious piece of stone—Mexican marble about two feet long and a foot wide. It bore upon its face a beautiful mountain landscape. The picture was of a mountain river winding along at the foot of high and rocky cliffs. Above the cliffs were precipitous mountains clothed half way to the top with pine trees and stunted shrubs. In one place, there were small rapids in the river and in another place its surface was as smooth as a mirror. The outline of the mountains and cliffs, and even of the verdure, was distinctly shadowed in the still water. The shimmer of the sun on the surface of the river and the white spray of the rapids were plainly brought out. A large pine tree stood at the top of a cliff, and was so perfect in detail that its roots clinging in the clefts of the rock could be seen. When the sun shone on the marble and brought out the colours, the picture looked as if an artist had painted it on the stone. However, in gas or electric light, the colours could not be seen.

The strangely beautiful stone was given to Colonel Hawley by Major Knappen, who owned the quarry in New Mexico where it was found. Major Knappen was the authority for the statement that the picture in the marble was an exact reproduction of the scenery on the side of the valley opposite where the quarry was located. The mountain peaks in the background of the landscape were the sentinels of the Guadaloupe range, and the river was the Riopenasis. (*Photographed by Nature*, 1890).

Grizzly Bear on Stone

An American paper said that it might be as well to warn not only evil-doers, but also respectable persons, male and female generally, to be careful what they were doing in a thunderstorm, or they might find themselves indelibly photographed by lightning on surrounding objects. A curious instance of this was found in a Photographic Gallery in Colorado Springs, belonging to a Mr. Guernsey, where a photograph of the figure of a bear on the rock was exhibited. The history of this 'great natural curiosity' is as follows:

"In the county of Bent, on the Purgatoire River, eighteen miles from Las Animas, Colorado, on the smooth face of a sandstone cliff overhung by a wall of rock, a hundred or more feet high, was found a life-size photograph of a grizzly bear. The picture was not an accidental resemblance to the animal, but a portrait more perfect and lifelike than any human art can supply. The short tail standing straight out, the ears visible, the mouth open, with eyes and teeth plainly to be seen, the attitude not constrained but perfectly natural, all demonstrated beyond the shadow of a doubt that the picture was a photograph stroke of lightning during the progress of a storm." (*Otago Witness*, 1875).

No one knew then in 1871, when the story first was related in a Pueblo newspaper, and no one knows even today, who or what impressed that picture on the rock. For it was no painting, no sculpture; yet its lifelike color stained the rock for a quarter of an inch in depth. (*Splitter*, 1955).

SNAPSHOTS OF PEOPLE ON GLASS AND OTHER OBJECTS

Young Lady's Picture on a Japanese Tray

A remarkable incident shows the sensitiveness of lacquered tin to flashes of lightning.

"On the evening of July 18[1886], Miss Lilliam Paul, of Plainfield, New Jersey, sat up alone at a late hour awaiting the return of a belated servant. A terrible thunderstorm was raging out and Miss Paul, fearing that the metal tray which rested near an open window would attract the lightning, stepped to place it in a more secluded spot. As she did so, she was startled by a wonderfully vivid flash of lightning, and hurriedly drew back. Timidly advancing again, she threw over the tray a rug, to secure it from the lightning. The next morning, on removing the rug, the pretty profile of Miss Paul was discovered fired upon the lacquered Japan tray. Since then experiments were made by experts to produce similar effects on lacquered trays, but without success." (*Instantaneous Photography by Lightning*, 1886).

The incidents attending this phenomenon are best described in the following statement which Mrs. Paul had prepared.

"I have been requested to given an account of a singular phenomenon or freak of nature that occurred in our house during the recent thunder storm, on the evening of the 18th July[1886]. The family had all retired early with the exception of my daughter, who was sitting up awaiting the arrival of a servant who was expected home any minute. The violence of the storm increased and the lightning was so vivid and continuous that there seemed to be no cessation between the flashes. My daughter, on stepping into the dining room to close the windows, saw that a small tray that lay upon a table in the bay window was attracting the lightning in what seemed a dangerous manner, being in the centre of an almost constant blaze of light. Approaching for the purpose of removing it, she was suddenly startled by a fearful flash and hastily turned away, but waiting for a few moments for an opportunity, she succeeded in drawing it off and covering it with a rug. Nothing further was thought of this until next morning, when, on removing it. We discovered a profile likeness of my daughter, apparently burned into the lacquer of the tray. We cannot account for this, except on the hypothesis that the picture must have been photographed by the electric light at the time my daughter drew back so suddenly."

(*The Chatham Courier*, November 10, 1886).

Mr. Leo Doft, the inventor of the electrical motor which bore his name, held that 'the picture was printed by light and not by heat, and that the flash was reflected from the face to the inside of the opposite window pane, and then thrown upon the tray, producing an actinic portrait'.

Faces on a Window Pane

On a Tuesday morning in July 1878, early-rising citizens of Santa Ana were startled to behold the face of some unknown person on the window glass of the office of Doctor Elffindorf, a local dentist. More extraordinary still, gradually a second spectra face made its appearance on the adjoining pane, and by six o'clock in the evening the two faces were visible from the opposite side of the road. "There they still are," said the reporter, "and as to the Doctor, he says he has seen such faces before. What he means by that, he refuses to say."

These mysterious faces in the window at Santa Ana reminded the editor of a like occurrence he had witnessed in San Francisco some three or four years earlier. At the time, he said, the lineaments of mysterious faces had appeared on the window panes of a house on Mason Street, near North Beach. Large crowds gathered to see the phenomena. The faces were unmistakably there but unaccounted for. Many theories were broached: there were flaws in the glass, they were photographs of passing people, taken by the unaided sun (this also was during the dry season).

The faces remained indelible in the glass day after day. Finally Mr. Woodward, owner of the well-known Woodward's Gardens, a local recreational enterprise and museum, bought one of the panes for $500, putting it on display for the edification of astonished crowds. When standing at a certain angle with this pane, the spectator could plainly see therein the face of an old man.

A woman's face appeared indelibly on window glass in Lawrence, Massachusetts, as told by Charles Fort in Books 960. The occupant of this house was so annoyed by the crowds of sightseers that, not having succeeded in washing off the picture, he finally removed the window sash.

Difficult to account for is the mysterious appearance and disappearance of a face on a window pane at New Albany, Indiana, in 1891. On December 2, 1891, a Mrs. Sophia Scharf, wife of

Anton Scharf, had died at her home at East Fifth and Spring Streets, New Albany. The funeral took place several days later. Shortly thereafter, Mrs. Frank Zoeller, a daughter-in-law of the dead woman, residing at East Eighth and Sycamore, came to the house and was surprised, even horrified, to observe on a front window a perfect representation of the head of her deceased mother-in-law.

Following this, the apparition seems to have vanished but after a time it reappeared, this time to stay. This reappearance coincided with a visit of Mrs. Peter Weinman, Fritz Weinman, two daughters of Officer Dennis Gleason, and various others. Several persons attempted to rub it off, by different means, without success.

Another example comes from *Scientific American Supplement* (1904). The image of a lady's face at her bedroom window watching a thunderstorm was said to be flashed onto the window pane. After many years, the impression gradually faded away, perhaps by erosion of the glass surface.

Four Faces on Glass

However curious the above may seem, there is more, as the following incident related by *Charlottesville Chronicle* (April 30, 1880) attests:

"We have heretofore published an account of a portrait supposed to have been photographed by lightning on a pane of glass in the window of an old farm house in this country. Another instance of the same curious phenomenon has been found in the window of the Mansion House on the 'Mount Eagle', far more generally known on the 'Gentry Place.'

The portraits of four persons are plainly discernible—two men, a woman and a child. The faces are not all on one pane, that of one of the men and the woman being an adjoining glasses, the face of the other man on another, and that of the child on one of the lower panes; and the theory is that the party were all looking through the

window during a thunderstorm, when a sudden flash of lightning, by some mysterious process, instantaneously fixed their features on the glass.
(*The Interior Journal*, 1880).

Family Photo on the Window

I.N. Brown, M.D., relates the following curious incident.

"The Nicholas Building is a corner building of two stories and forms an 'L' fronting on the two streets. The upper story has been occupied in whole or in part by families or as workshops in the inverse order as follows.

John M. Wilson, present occupant lacking, Charles Day, John McKinley, B.W. Day's Shoe and harness shop, Jas (James) Wm. (William) Boyce, John Mofford, Jack Boyce, the Grange etc. On the rear of each L in the upper story there is a window facing respectively southwest and northwest. Last January 1880, O.W. Davis accidentally discovered a distinct likeness of a little girl's face on one of the panes of the window facing southwest. The attention of several persons was called to it at the time, each of whom saw the face, but for reasons best known to themselves it was not made public until last Monday evening. On Tuesday morning considerable interest seemed to be manifested about the matter, when my attention was first called to it. Armed with John L Barkley's *opera glass*, I began an investigation of what was to be seen, and on examination, the likeness of a little girl was distinctly seen on the window pane, or rather, appeared a little inside the window, so distinct indeed that all the party there present, some twenty in number, agreed that it was the likeness of Cora Rogers, a little daughter of Thos. Rogers. This child, about six years old, lived with Jas. W. Boyce, who occupied these rooms about a year and a half ago.

On careful inspection another image was discovered on the same pane. The face turned partly toward the observer. And on the other side of the first picture, still another much stronger but plump and smiling and later in the day still a fourth one; this was of an older person, all on the same pane. None of these last could be identified. Viewed from a particular locality, and under favorable circumstances of illumination, all the first three could be seen at once. The fourth seemed to partly overlap the others, and could not always be seen at the same time with the others.

While looking at this object, one of the company, Mrs. Ln. Carter, discovered what was supposed to be another likeness on one of the panes of the other window (the one facing northwest). Almost all could see it, but by means of the *opera glass* I found no difficulty in recognizing the faces of two children lying abed, the face of one partly concealed from view by the one in front. Several of the party could recognize this also. Later in the day, Dr. O. D. Simmons discovered another face on the same pane, and still later I found the fourth one, all four distinctly seen under favourable circumstances at one view.

At one time in the forenoon, the sash was removed to within the darkened room, but by even so careful management of the light the views were not as satisfactory as in its natural place in the window.

Later in the afternoon, I could distinctly recognize a likeness on another pane of this last window, and also Walter Simmons discovered a good likeness on still another pane of the same window. With the *opera glass*, I could plainly see this face. It was that of a little girl with a round-crowned hat on. This made four panes of window glass having on them these likenesses.

They are viewed from the ground and from many positions and distances. A good deal depends on their illumination and the particular point from which they are viewed. By placing a dark hat behind the picture it is shown in the hat.

Nothing can be discovered on or in the pane of window-glass when very close to it. The panes were washed and rubbed dry etc. only to make the images more distinct, doubtless by removing particles of dust etc.

Later (Wednesday noon), on the pane first described today, on carefully focusing the *opera glass* in steady position and in particular locality, and in good state of personal health and fasting, I was enabled to see it appear literally full of faces. I countered nine of men beside the children first described. They could not all be seen at one view, but all from some locality. In directing the point of vision to this or that locality, I would see the image there; the others would gradually dissolve away. They seemed to overlap each other somewhat like a lot of coin thrown promiscuously in a heap.

It is known that Grange had a meeting in this room on one particularly electric night. Now, how came these pictures here? Evidently they were photographed by lightning. The flash of lightning furnished the light to form the image, and this, together with the accompanying electricity, produced chemical or molecular change in the constituents of the glass and then the images were fixed."
(*Utah Journal*, 1880).

Death Scene Pictured in a Glass Pane

On the afternoon of August 7, 1908, W. Goree was standing in the front door of his home on Ninth Avenue, West New Decatur, watching a heavy electrical storm. His wife was standing near his side. A stroke of lightning instantly killed Mr. Goree and seriously shocked his wife, but she recovered. A bed within the house on which two children slept was torn into kindling wood, but the children were unhurt.

There was a large glass in the front door, where Mr. Goree was standing when killed, and it was later discovered that there was a perfect picture on the glass which was photographed by the lightning flash. In the picture, Mr. Goree was shown with his head slightly upturned, as if watching the storm cloud. A large fig bush which stood in the yard was also shown, and a portion of the yard fence also appeared. A house and a small tripe of woods, fully a quarter of a mile away, were shown in the picture as were also two telephone poles about 100 yards from the house. Plainer than all was the picture of Mrs. Goree. She was shown with her lips slightly parted as if in the act of speaking. The bolt of lightning which killed Mr. Goree and seriously shocked Mrs. Goree was also plainly photographed on the glass. The picture was on exhibition in the *Decatur News* Office and attracted considerable attention (*Times Daily*, 1908).

Another Picture on a Window Pane

The New York Times (October 14, 1883), carried the following incident reportedly published by *Charlottesville Chronicle*.

"A gentleman informed the Editor that while coming to town in his wagon, his little son called his attention to a picture which he said he saw in a window of the house on University-avenue occupied by N. G. Clifton. He got down from his wagon and examined the window, and found upon a pane of glass an excellent photograph likeness of the Late Mrs. Bowyer, the mother of Mrs. Clifton. The family had never noticed the picture but recollected that many years ago Mrs. Bowyer, at the occurrence of a severe storm, while seated near the window had been somewhat shocked by lightning."

(*Another Picture on a Window-Pane*, 1883).

Other Images on Glass, Lens and Mirror

Rainbow on Window Pane

Equally strange, although in small proportions, was the appearance of a permanent rainbow on an ordinary window pane in Kentucky. It was in full color, perfect in every detail.

"Jesse Smith, an elderly farmer, had lived six miles west of Demossville, Kentucky, all during the Civil War, having been in residence there since 1857. There was nothing out of the ordinary about his window until the early spring of 1865, just before the close of the war. Suddenly, after a severe storm the strange phenomenon appeared—a rainbow about six inches wide, extended from one side of the window to the other, involving all three panes of the lower sash. The colors from the top downward were yellow, orange, red, purple, blue, green, yellow, orange, red, violet—the blue and green varying somewhat, in position, from the natural. The colors were bright, clear and plainly visible as far as 50 yards from the house. Singularly, however, it was visible only from the outside of the house. From within not a tinge of color was noticeable. The rainbow was in the glass and not an illusion, for on hoisting the sash the rainbow moved with the glass.

When the rainbow first appeared on the glass it created a near-panic in the neighborhood, for at that critical period it seemed to many that the phantom bow must foretell some dreadful calamity. Indeed, a Southerner might have seen his fears realized when, soon after, General Lee was forced to surrender and the Southern cause collapsed. Mr. Smith was advised to remove the sash but, being either less superstitious or more fatalistic than most, he left it where it was. Almost 20 years later, in the summer of 1882, the rainbow was as brilliant as ever and its story appeared in *The Cincinnati Enquirer* that year."

(*Splitter*, 1955).

Snapshot on Survey Lens

"In the summer of 1854, a land survey was being made in San Joaquin County, California, during the course of which a surveyor's instrument was left standing in the hot sun while the men ate their lunch. The instrument was set facing a woodland. When the men came back they found imprinted on its front lens a beautiful landscape in natural colors. The woodland and details of the surrounding landscape were as real as in life. This phenomenon was reported in 1869 by *Tuolumne City News.*" (*Splitter*, 1955).

The other instance was more noticeable and worthy of mention. It was reported in 1878 from the Death Valley area, just across the mountains from the San Joaquin. Field glasses which were supposed to have belonged to Hahn, a lost guide to Wheeler's expedition had been found in the desert near Death Valley. They were brought into town by an Indian. Every object within range of where the glasses had lain for a year was distinctly outlined or 'photographed' upon both of the object lenses. On both glasses were, so to say, etched by a master hand the nearby desert shrubs, with branches, twigs, and leaves in the utmost and meticulous detail. There was no fuzziness of outline, all being distinctly traced upon the clear glass. The picture seemed to occupy approximately the centre of each of the object glasses, though perhaps a little nearer the plane that the convex side. The editor of the *Inyo Independent* (*Independence, California*), who talked of the incident, remarked that he had heard of such phenomena before but this was one of the most striking examples.

"Another one of those rare instances in which lightning had drawn a photograph upon glass was reported in the year 1895 from an observatory situated on Mount Arie, near the summer resort of West Baden. One of the astronomers of that institution on making an examination of the object glass of one of the telescopes was surprised to find a perfect photograph of a flower upon both lenses of the instrument. It was believed that the photograph was drawn by lightning, the glass having been left exposed during a storm on one of the upper platforms of the observatory. The flower was one known only in the Mount Arie district." (*Aurora Daily Express*, 1895).

A similar incident happened at a house near Deal (England) during a thunderstom. The lightning imprinted a perfect photograph of a flower vase on a mirror before which it stood. (*The Rice belt journal*, 1907).

Window Glass Portraits and Haunted Houses

"Reputedly, [the so-called] haunted houses sometimes contain lightning window-glass portraits. An elderly Mrs. Rodman, living in a New York town, several years prior to 1892, was killed by lightning in her home. About a month later, the daughter of the deceased woman was passing the house where her mother had lived, when she saw her mother's face in one of the windows. The house at once was said to be haunted. For almost a year the face was not seen but one day a citizen of the town passing by saw the face once more. It did not change as he approached. Upon investigation, he found that the dead woman's likeness was imprinted on the pane of glass. It appeared there very faintly, it is true, and it was noticeable only when the sun was in a certain position, but nonetheless it was universally declared to be the most lifelike portrait of Mrs. Rodman ever seen. (*Splitter*, 1955).

There was a house in Washington, D.C., said to be haunted by the ghosts of its former occupants, Commodore Meade and his mother. After their death, many persons declared they saw ghosts about the place. No servants lived there. Finally the palatial house was rented. Mr. Smith, the lessee, one day gave a great dinner. The guests wandered about, praising the size and beauty of the rooms. One of the men, glancing through the long plate glass window of the back parlor overlooking the garden in the rear, started, dropped his cigar, and turning to Mr. Smith, his host, exclaimed, "Look there!" One after another of those present stared at the window. "Why, there is the old Commodore, big as life! And his mother!" they exclaimed. "By all that's holy!" said the host. "That's Meade! Dead long ago." Scarcely waiting to give their excuses, the guests rushed for the cloakroom and speedily left.

Mr. Smith had the glass examined. An expert from New York copied the faces. A committee of photographers waited upon the best electricians, the electricians waited upon the scientists of the Smithsonian Institution. Scientists cut out the pane of glass, thereby preserving the impressions.

The conclusion of all this investigation was as follows: The panes were of the finest French plate glass brought from overseas more than 100 years previously. They were made of flinten sand and possessed a softer, finer finish than glass made at a later date. Most important, it seemed, of all, was the recollection that Commodore Meade and his aged mother had shortly before their death been sitting near this window during a violent thunderstorm. They had thus been photographed upon the glass, as the reporter put it, "by a brilliant flash light from the heavens by a process known only to the Maker of all mankind." (*Splitter*, 1955)

Old Lady in her Cap and Gown

"There is a story from the little Tennessee village of Ooltewah, on the road from Chattanooga to Cleveland. In 1887, a crowd of people gathered at a humble farmhouse by the roadside and a passerby, asking the meaning of the assemblage, was told, "Old Mrs. Osborne is dead." This lady, the mother of Farmer Osborne, had been bed-ridden for many years. Shortly before her death, Mrs. Osborne, lying in her bed near the window in the same little room she had occupied for years, watched a terrific thunderstorm come up. As she lay in bed she saw the lightning strike and shiver to fragments a tall pine tree standing nearby. She was so frightened that she rapidly sank into unconsciousness and only lingered on until the next day when she died. When the neighbors came to lay her out, they discovered to the great astonishment of all, and the dismay of many, that on one of the eight by 10-inch panes in the window beside her bed was a photographic likeness of the old lady in her neat cap and gown." (*Splitter*, 1955).

A correspondent of *Savannah News* decided to verify the authenticity of the news by making a personal visit to the spot. Before his visit, he was thinking that some sort of superstitions, aided by the vivid imagination of the spectators might have contorted into some sort of fancied resemblance, just as we may discover shapes in the fleeting clouds. But what was his surprise instead to see, not an imperfect pane of glass but a perfect one, on

which was plainly visible a faint, though perfect, picture of an old woman in cap and gown lying in bed. In his words, "the picture was there, and though not distinct or highly enough finished to have been delivered to a customer by a first-class photographer, it was certainly a correct photographic likeness, unfinished on that glass by some natural process, and not by the hand of man, and remains a mystery for science to solve.
(*Fortworth Daily Gazette*, 1887).

The "Russellville Girl"

Russellville is located in the far south-west corner of the state, but the fate of the "Russellville Girl" has been told in every corner of Kentucky. The story goes that a young girl was waiting for her lover to pick her up one night for a dance. It was a stormy and dangerous night, as lightning illuminated the sky and rain fell in sheets. She was very anxious about her boy friend's driving in such weather and stood near the front window of the house, anxiously watching the dark road outside and hoping for some sign of his oncoming headlights. Just then a bolt of lightning struck the house and somehow passed through the front window, instantly killing the girl.

In the days followed, no one seemed able to remember just what this girl's name might have been, but they didn't have any trouble remembering what she looked like. By some freak of nature, the lightning created a photographic imprint of the girl on the pane of glass in the front window.

For many years, on every occasion when it rained, the girl's image would appear on the glass. The story became famous and people came from miles around to see the image. No matter how hard the owners cleaned the window, they could not erase the imprint. As years passed, the window was boarded over to keep away the curiosity seekers. More recently, it has been painted over.

The house where the girl's image was imprinted on the window is a private home on Clarksville road. It later served as the residence for the caretaker of Maple Grove Cemetery. Recently, in the year 2009, Russellville Mayor Gene Zick ordered the west window of the building to be cleaned of the paint. (*Window cleared on the Sexton House; Lightning tale resurrected*, 2009).

A similar story was related in the *Western Electrician* under the title *"Photographed by Lightning"* referring to a religious paper published at Waterloo, Iowa and stated that it came from a reliable source.

"A strange freak of electricity occurred in Thayer County, Nebraska, a state on the Great Plains of the Midwestern United States during a storm. Miss Annie Holsinger had gone to the well for water and upon returning to the house saw, as she supposed, her mother looking at her through a window. She thought nothing of this; but when later she went to the well and saw her mother again watching her, she was much perplexed, especially as she found her mother sitting just as she had been when the daughter left the room. Upon investigation it was found that Mrs. Holsinger had not left her chair, and that which the daughter had seen was a life-size picture on the window pane. It had been photographed there by the lightning. The portrait remained for a few days on the glass and then faded away."
(*Photographed by Lightning*, 1892).

Widow Claimed her Husband's 'Negative'

The following sentimental story appeared in the *Kentucky News Era* on November 20, 1913.

The widow of 'Monk' Russell made a trip to Spottsville to get the pane of glass on which it was believed lightning photographed the image of her deceased husband. She carried it to her home at Chandler, Indiana, with the intention of preserving the glass as a curious memento.

'Monk' Russell was a miner of Spottsville and was shocked by a stroke of lightning while sitting at the window. He died a short time later and then it was found there was a picture of him left on the glass. According to Henderson Gleaner who reported the incident, the glass appeared like an old-fashioned wet-plate negative (*Kentucky News Era*, 1913).

Another Window Pane Picture

The stories of mysteriously appearing portraits on window panes have been vouched once more by the following from the *Charlottesville (Va.) Chronicle* published in the year 1875.

"Within the last two weeks a singular discovery has been made at the house of Jesse Garth, for many years deceased. It is said that a distinct and accurate likeness of Mrs. Garth, who has been dead for twenty years, can be seen on a pane of glass in the upper sash of one of the windows, presenting very much the appearance of a photographic negative. The discovery is said to have been made by a woman who was washing clothes in the yard, who imagined someone was watching her through the window and went inside to see who it was. We gather these facts from Dr. Charles Brown, who has himself seen the singular picture. Dr. Brown remembers that about twenty years ago Mr. Garth told him that his wife while standing at that window was stunned by a sudden flash of lightning and the Doctor's theory is that the outlines of her features were photographed on the window pane at that time. The youngest daughter of Mr. Garth and others who were well acquainted with Mrs. Garth have seen the picture and pronounce it a striking likeness. It is said to be more distinct about nine o'clock in the morning and three on the afternoon than at any other times of the day."
(*Gallipolis Journal*, 1875).

Face in the Courthouse Window

Perhaps the most interesting and best authenticated case of lightning photography is that associated with Carrollton, Alabama where an ex-slave by the name of Henry Wells was imprisoned in the year 1876 after he admitted setting fire to the Pickens County Court-house. There are several versions of this story, but the most prevalent one is that Wells was hidden in an upper story of the courthouse after report reached the sheriff that he might be lynched. One stormy night, as the frightened Negro peered down into the public square, he thought he saw a mob gathering and at the height of his terror a bolt of lightning ripped the sky and photographed his fear-crazed face upon the window-pane. This image in the glass remained a public curiosity in the Carrollton for many years.

Finally, in the year 1940, the Carrollton Civil Club investigated and issued the following official explanation of the strange event:

"While Wells was standing at the window, looking upon the mob below, the unusually bright flash of lightning struck. This was a case of lightning photography, for it stamped the prisoner's features indelibly on the window pane." (Alabama: A Guide to the Deep South, 1941)

Station Homestead on Window Pane

The Sydney Morning Herald, December 3, 1940 edition, carried the following story entitled "Strange Effect of Lightning—'Picture' Traced on Window."

During a violent storm at Moree, New South Wales, Australia, lightning made tracings on the window of a house which, the town people declared, has a picture of a station homestead 20 miles away. When the report of this phenomenon was referred to the State Meteorologist, Mr. Mares, he said, "I have read of lightning making impressions and pictures, although no instance has ever come directly to my notice. These 'pictures' have generally been of leaves or trees. I have never read of a picture being imprinted on a window but apparently it is some sort of freakish effect of lightning. Whether it is really a reflection of real objects is, as far as I know, merely a matter of conjecture."

The description of the impression on the glass given in the report from Moree is: "The picture appears to be of a station homestead at Gurley more than 20 miles away. The picture shows outbuildings, cattle and sheep". It was suggested that the unusual window pane might be a photographic negative, but the occupier of the house said that she had been in the house for eight years and had never noticed the picture until after the storm. (*Strange Effect of Lightning*, 1940).

Images within a Larger Image

"Remarkable Effect of Lightning" published in the *London Literary Gazette*, January 1820 read as follows:

"About twenty years ago, during a violent thunder storm, the lightning struck a pane of glass in a house door, so that the mistress of the house, who was in the hall behind the door was cast several paces backwards and thrown on the floor. She however received no injury, nor was the pane of glass broken. The electric fluid had however left upon it a beautiful painting (if we may so express it) resembling, on the whole a head, which was formed of numerous smaller heads."
(*Francis*, 1820).

Mrs. Evans Attestation to the Phenomenon

Mrs. Augusta Evans Wilson (1835-1909), the famous American writer and a literary genius, was very proud of her use of the lightning photographic phenomenon in her novels. In the novel '*At the Mercy of Tiberius*', the heroin Beryl Brentano is accused of murdering her grandfather. Although absolutely innocent, she refuses to defend herself for fear of implicating her brother. However both Beryl and her brother are absolved of the charges because of a lightning photograph that had been imprinted on the windowpane revealing that a bolt of lightning had killed the grandfather. She wrote a friend that she could afford to laugh at reviewers who ridiculed the incident of lightning making imprints of surrounding objects. She said, she, before writing the novel, had carefully investigated the electrical phenomenon and had collected accounts of four or five well-authenticated instances of faces photographed on window panes by flashes of lightning. One instance of lightning photography took place in the house of Mrs. Wilson's uncle, Dr. Novborne B. Powell of Chunnenuggee Ridge, Alabama, in about the year 1873. Relatives testified that the image of Dr. Powell's wife was photographed on a pane of glass during a severe electrical storm. Mrs. Powell's distinctive cap and her large cameo pin were recognizable in the picture, we are told. In the year 1911, the glass was purchased by a grandson of the lady in the miraculous image, Dr. Edward H. Carry, who served as the President of the American Medical Association and President of Southwestern Medical College. Dr. Carry kept the glass for several years and then repented its removal from Alabama. In about the year 1920, he sent the glass to the Alabama Department of Archives, but shortly thereafter it was shattered beyond repair. (*Fidler*, 2003). Later letters of apology came to Mrs. Wilson from people who had seen these remarkable pictures.

Sallie May Boundy and her Research

Mrs. Sallie May Boundy was famously referred to as the 'lightning bug' because she used to collect photographs made by lightning and had travelled in all parts of the United States for many years searching for instances of lightning photography and researching on the subject. She found that when this unusual phenomenon occurs on clear glass, such as a window, it remains permanently. She found such an image in Georgia. It was the picture of an old Negro man and a perfect likeliness. Altogether she had discovered as many as 35 instances of lightning photography. An interesting one was on the inside of a big wash pot which depicted the immediate sourroundings in which the pot stood (*The Miami News*, 1953).

Interestingly, Sallie when she was a child, had her picture pritned on a mirror in the front hall of the Edmonson home in Eufaula, Alabama. The picture remained for several days and then faded out. She was so intriqued by this experience that in later years she investigated every report of lightning photography. (D.K. Wilgus, 1970).

Recent Images

The Miraculous Appearance of Virgin Mary on a Window Pane

Alex Leiva was working at his job at Olden Avenue Car Wash. One day in October 2012, when cleaning up the parking lot and getting ready for the day, he saw flashing lights and a cloud of smoke. Thinking the car wash was on fire, Leiva ran toward the building. Then the smoke cleared—and he saw the image of the Virgin Mary holding baby Jesus in the window of the car wash tunnel, he said. Leiva said he grabbed his camera phone from his belt holster and started snapping photos. He dropped the phone, and by the time he picked it up, the image was gone.
(*Behold the image of Blessed Virgin Mary seen in New Jersey*).

In the village of Absam, near Innsbruck, Austria, a special image of Our Lady suddenly appeared on a pane of glass in the home of the Bucher family in 1797. The image is in the glass and is not etched or painted. If the pane of glass is immersed in water the image disappears but then re-appears when the glass dries. This miraculous image of Our Lady of Absam, not made by human hands (acheropite) is now enshrined in the local church for over 200 years (*Our Lady of Absam*).

The miraculous image of Our Lady of Absam can be seen even today in a side altar of the parish church of Absam. The glass pane is just seven inches tall and five inches wide, but the face of Mary can be clearly seen. It is enclosed in a metal shrine with golden rays, a golden crown, golden flowers, and precious jewels. The face of the Virgin in the image is young and gentle and befits the most affectionate title used commonly by Austrians and Germans for the Virgin Mary: 'Our Dear Lady' (*Shrine of Our Lady of Absam*)

Truck with Image of Jesus

In October, 2009, Jim Stevens of Jonesborough, Tennessee spotted an image resembling Jesus Christ on the driver side window of his Isuzu pickup truck. Since then, whenever there is morning dew, the visage reappears only to vanish in the day when the dew evaporates. Jim has tried tolling the window up and down but that has not stopped the image reappearing.

Image of Mary in Malaysian Hospital

On November 20, 2012, an image resembling the Virgin Mary at a Church of Our Lady of Lourdes at the port town of Klang (on the outskirts of Kaula Lumpur) appeared on a window pane of a Malaysian hospital. The window pane located in the seventh floor of the hospital has been shifted to a Church after attracting crowds of devout Catholics and curious visitors. This incidence has been reported widely in the media across the world. However, it has failed to attract the attention of the scientists.

The supposed Virgin Mary sighting happened at Sime Darby Medical Centre (SDMC) in Subang Jaya, Selangor, outside Kaula Lumpur
Image courtesy:www.freemalaysiatoday.com

Face of Jesus on Tree Stump

Belfast Telegraph carried the following story in its 9th August 2012 edition.

The stump is from a recently-felled tree beside a grave in Belfast City Cemetery in west Belfast. A video of the mysterious image has been posted to YouTube, with the message:

"An image has appeared on a tree stump in Belfast's City Cemetery. Upon close inspection, it's hard to tell just how this image got there. Recently some employees of the City Council trimmed trees in the cemetery and as a result this phenomenon appeared." (*Belfast Telegraph*, 2012).

Life-Like Image of a Lady in Urbana Coffee Shop

"Streetcap on Bay Street in front of Urbana Coffee as photographed by
Miguel Horitiguela, Toronto photographer serving Toronto, GTA and
Southern Ontario"
Copyright©Miguel Horitiguela

Mr. Miguel Horitiguela is a professional photographer serving
Toronto, GTA and Southern Ontario. During a head out for the
busy sidewalks and laneways in search of a photographic scene, he
captured the above image in the front glass doors of Urbana Coffee
shop located on Bay Street. He was completely unaware that there
was a smiling face on the glass when he took the photograph.
During processing of the photograph, he identified the face and
enlarged it.

Mystery face appears in pub's window

Drinkers in one Shropshire bar have been left scratching their heads after a series of spooky goings on—including a face appearing on the bar's window.

Staff and punters at the White Hart pub in Iron Bridge might have been accused of drinking one too many ales until one customer snatched this picture on his mobile phone. Bar manager Mike Herbert said that they do not know what it is and added the pub has never seen anything like it before. One person said it looked like Elvis Presley, the famous American singer and actor.

4

MISDIAGNOSIS OF OBSERVATIONS

Miracles happen, not in opposition to Nature, but in opposition to what we know of Nature

—St. Augustine

At all times, new discoveries have encountered violent opposition. Facts were denied because they did not fit into the theories prevailing at the time. Every truth has had its opponents and every falsehood its supporters. Sometimes, truth is overcome by falsehood, but it is temporary and not permanent. As Herbert Spencer has said, every falsehood has some remote connection with the truth, to say the least. Often the truth gets buried in the archives of half-backed theories. This is what happened in the case of lightning photographs also. Theorists of the time failed to distinguish between the tree-like dentric patterns caused by lightning on the body of its victims and the life-like images of adjacent objects and portraits of human faces on window panes etc. They painted all the cases of lightning imprints with the same brush.

Although in the majority of cases the photographs resembled trees, there was one case in which it resembled a horse-shoe; another, a cow; a third, a piece of furniture; a fourth, the entire surrounding landscape and so on.

In this chapter, we will explore how the misinterpretation of facts and observations led to incorrect conclusions which helped the skeptics to propagate a false impression that the lightning imprints are nothing but *Lichtenberg* figures and lightning *per se* has no photographic qualities. The error was in fact due to a mixing up of facts. Let's examine the issue in detail.

In the 19th century, the phenomenon of lightning moved from the realm of the supernatural into the burgeoning domains of natural science (physics), and a vigorous debate ensued about whether a flash of lightning could transfer an image of the vicinity of the strike onto adjacent bodies and objects. The phenomenon was given a name: *keranography* (sometimes referred to as *ceraunography* or *keraunography*), a combination from the Greek suggesting 'writing or drawing with lightning.' (*Rickard*).

There do seem to be periods when lightning figures are explained according to what Charles Fort called the 'dominants of the age', theories favoured by the savants of the day. In the 19th century, we find photography used as the best analogy. Suddenly we find no more 'crosses' but a more sophisticated configuration likened to 'flowers'. For example, Flammarion speaks of a woman struck by lightning which left "the likeness of a flower imprinted on her leg." He explains that this was possibly because "a flower had stood in the route of the discharge". It seems this phenomenon was well known as 'Lichtenberg flowers' to doctors who treated the victims. Rudolph Golde, a British pioneer of lightning research in the mid-1900s, told Frank Lane that the markings should properly be called 'Lichtenberg figures' as they "have been known to physicists for many decades before the true nature of the markings found on bodies was explained to the medical fraternity" (*Rickard*).

These 'Lichtenberg figures' were first identified in laboratory by German physicist Georg Lichtenberg and therefore the branching, root-like dendritic patterns of electric discharges were named after him.

In a paper read by Prof. C. Tomlinson of King's College before the physical section of the British Association at Manchester in 1861, he showed that the ramified figures so often observed on the bodies of lightning victims were not derived from any tree, whatever, but represent the fiery hand of the lightning itself. He exhibited some of these figures as produced by the discharge of a Leyden jar, and it was generally allowed that the resemblance to a tree was sufficient to lead an ordinary observer to connect the ramified figure found on the body of a person struck by lightning with the tree under which he sought refuge. Thus, when the 'photographic properties' of lightning was strenuously advocated by the observers of these natural phenomenon, scientists advanced the theory that the floral impressions occasionally made by lightning were not photographic reproduction of the trees or leaves, but the pattern of electric discharge produced by lightning. Though the advocates of the theory were right in their argument, they failed to distinguish between the tree-like images and other photographic reproduction of images (un-tree-like images).

Bob Rickard, in an article *'Tattoos from the Blue—People branded by lightning'* which appeared in the *Fortean times*, has analyzed the problem in the right perspective. He quite rightly pointed out that there were a remarkable number of accounts of quite **un-tree-like** images. Poey mentions that the image of a palm-leaf hut and its surroundings was found etched on some dried leaves at San Vicente, Cuba; and Steinmetz notes a 'perfectly engraved image of a cow' on the body of a woman who was tending it when it was struck by lightning. Moreover, no simple photographic process could explain the curious selection by which, say, a tree is imprinted but not the rest of the scene; and also, how the images were transmitted *through* the victim's (often heavy and opaque) clothing.

Nevertheless, it is an acceptable fact that some of the trees (pine tree, for example) resemble the 'dendritic' pattern occasionally found imprinted on the body of the lightning victims. This floral pattern of electric discharge due to lightning can be seen in the following photograph.

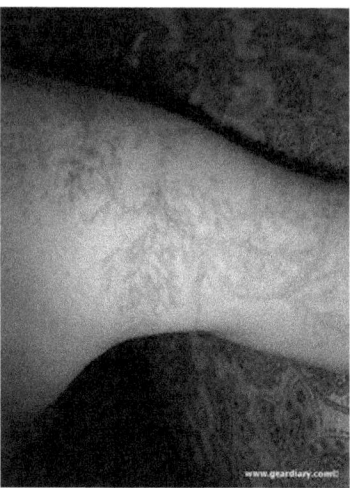

Dendritic pattern on the arms of a lightning victim
Image Courtesy: www.geardiary.com

Readers can easily observe that the dendritic patterns that appeared on the lightning-victims are more or less similar to the pattern of poplar trees—a form of fractal lines

One dimension of the problem is solved if one carefully observes the similarity between these patterns because almost all the cases relating to imprint of trees (the branching pattern of which are similar to the dendritic pattern of lightning imprints) can be catalogued into this class of the so-called 'Lichtenberg flowers' or 'Lichtenberg figures'. It has been thus rightly contended by the medical fraternity that these imprints are not 'photographs' produced by the lightning, as once was thought. The real explanation probably is that a very weak current is subdivided by the resistance of the tissues, causing rupture of many superficial capillaries, or small blood-vessels, thus giving the 'tree-like arborisation.

There is yet another dimension to the problem, which the modern inquirers omitted in order to suit their convenience. This relates to the imprint of *un-tree-like* images with photograph-likeness.

Going by the numerous cases reported in the local newspapers and other works spread over more than two centuries, we are given to understand that everyday's observation of the nature's operations is totally neglected; even where it is so conspicuous to attract the attention of mass of people, as it recently happened in the Malaysian hospital window where a purported image of Virgin Mary appeared. We are often too indolent to examine and find the reasons for ourselves.

5

MENTAL STIGMATA
AND BODILY IMPRINTS

An object making a violent impression on the mother's mind, its image is instantly projected into the astral light, or the universal ether, which Jevons and Babbage, as well as the authors of the Unseen Universe, tell us is the repository of the spiritual images of all forms and even human thoughts—H.P. Blavatsky

S trange as are the foregoing cases of lightning imprints, those of mental imprint of images and letters on the skin, eclipse them. There are various instances on record in which individuals have been said to have words (generally a name) pictorially marked upon the iris or on the surface of the skin. These manifestations usually witnessed on a person's skin are scientifically known as 'stigmata' or dermographism. Their importance for the present discussion lies mainly in their demonstration of the body's malleability and susceptibility to imprint of images on skin, and so as to make a basic understanding and acceptance of holographic nature of body and mind.

Readers may probably doubt the relevance of mental stigmata here in a book which mainly deals with the lightning imprints.

The purpose of inserting a chapter on mental stigmata is twofold. In both the cases, pictorial impressions appear on skin. So, the phenomenon of stigmatism demonstrates the body's malleability and susceptibility to imprint pictorial representations under appropriate conditions. A natural corollary to this is that the human body is susceptible to imprint of images brought by the electromagnetic waves emitted by lightning also.

Second, these phenomena attest the holographic nature of human body and of course, the entire universe. As per the holographic brain theory, the brain projects an image outside of itself. Russian psychologists Dr. Alexander P. Dubrov and Dr. Veniamin N. Pushkin have written extensively on the idea. To use their own words, "Records of ejection of psychophysical structures outside the brain would provide direct evidence of brain holograms."

In the following cases, the human mind, in some extreme conditions, create hologram-like field patterns of the thought-forms, which in turn get impressed on the body. These cases will demonstrate in clear terms that the field patterns created by the mind can accordingly modify the body-field and re-orient the molecules. Readers may, for easy understanding, compare the magnetic field created by a bar magnet which orients the iron-fillings placed near the magnetic field.

And if this be the case, the field-patterns of organic and inorganic objects, if supposed to be carried along by the electromagnetic waves emitted by lightning, can also modify the body-pattern of the victims and re-orient the bio-molecules in such a way that the geometric patterns they carried get imprinted on the skin/body. In other words, in the case of stigmata, the source of bodily imprints are 'thought-forms' created in the mind. In the case of lightning imprints, the source are 'wave-forms' of images carried by the coherent electromagnetic waves emitted by lightning.

Some of the curious cases where the thought-forms or mental images got imprinted on the body of the persons are discussed here.

Dr. Charles Baudouin of the Jean Jacques Roussequ Institute, Geneva, in his *'Suggestion and Auto-Suggestion'* (English translation, 1920), speaks of dermographism as a process of an image existing in the subject's mind that becomes outlined on the skin. He proceeds to cite from Dr. Charles Richet of Paris a well-known instance of dermographism.

A child, playing about the room idly loosens the catch which fastens a chimney draw-plate, and narrowly escapes being guillotined by the quick fall of the heavy steel-edged mechanism. The mother receives such a shock on seeing the danger that a flushing erythematous circle forms round her neck—the corresponding part was threatened in the case of the child and this remains swollen for several hours. Here we have a striking instance of the power of emotion. There is an enormous body of evidence for this kind of occurrence of unusual images or letters in the eye, skin and other parts of the body.

Cross Mark on a Girl's Arm

The New York Times, Dublin edition dated November 14, 1910 carried an extraordinary story on what is described as mysterious markings appearing upon the arm of a child boarding in the Kiltimargh Convent.

"According to the report in the news, the girl is thirteen, and has been a boarder at the Convent for three or four years. About three weeks ago, she was heard screaming loudly in her sleep. When interrogated she said she had had a fearful dream, in which she had seen the crucifixion. On the following morning she found her arm and wrist sore, and it was seen that her forearm was marked with a cross as were the letters "I.H.S". Some days later there appeared below the letters something that resembled a crown of thorns, and a little later above the cross the letters in scroll "I.N.R.I". Other markings are said to have appeared at a later period, extending from the wrist to the forearm. It is reported that the markings were examined by several people in the town."

A similar instance was reported in the London-based *Sunday News* (Aug. 3, 1926). Dorothy Parrot, 4-year-old child of R. S. Parrot, of Winget Mill, Georgia, was marked by a red spot on her body. Out of this spot formed three letters, *R. I. C.* Doctors could not explain this. (Fort, Wild Talents, 2004)

Another story appeared in *London Daily Express*, Nov. 17, 1913 related to the phenomena of a girl, aged 12, of the village of Bussus-Bus-Suel, near Abbeville, France. If asked questions, answers appeared in bold red letters on her arms, legs and shoulders. Also upon her body appeared pictures, such as of a ladder, a dog, a horse. (Fort, Wild Talents, 2004)

Dated Kitten

In May 1921, a cat belonging to Madame Davico, a baker in Nice, France, gave birth to four kittens, two gray, one white and one black. One gray kitten had the figure *'1921'* on its chest. The other had the same imprint, though not as distinct, on the abdomen. The figures, formed in dark gray hair, were plainly visible on the light gray background. In both cases three spots, similar to three stars, were visible just above the figures. Madame Davico related that some time before the birth of the kittens, the mother was chasing a mouse and jumped on a sack of flour. Thinking that the animal's claws might tear a hole in the sack, Madame Davico threw an empty sack over the full one. The disappointed cat waited several hours for the mouse to reappear, all the while staring the date 1921 with three stars above the figure. The kittens, born a few weeks later, had in their chest the number 1921! (*Tomorrow*, 1952).

Girl with Stigmatic Biting

"Girl with spirit of mischief" published in the *London Evening Standard* (October 1, 1926) reported that in September, 1926, a Rumanian girl, Eleanore Zugun, was taken to London for observation by the National Laboratory for Psychical Research.

Countess Wassilko-Serecki, who had taken the girl to London, said, in an interview (London *Evening Standard*, Oct. 1, 1926), that she had seen the word *Dracu* form upon the girl's arm. This word is the Rumanian word for the Devil.

As the story goes, when she was 11 years old, Eleanore Zugun visited her grandmother's house at Buhai, a few miles away from her village Talpa. On the way she found some money by the side of the road, and when she arrived at Buhai, she spent it on sweets and ate them all. Zugun's 105-year-old grandmother, who had the reputation of being a witch, overheard Eleanore and her cousin arguing about the sweets and warned her that the devil (Dracu in Rumanian) had left the money to tempt her, and from then on she would never be free of him. The next day stigmatic biting and scratches started appearing on her body.

Alleged Father's name Appears in Infant's Eyes

A similar instance was reported about 1825 by Dr. Munro of Edinburg who frequently exhibited a child in whose eyes many persons imagined they could read the name and age of his father.

"A young woman in Galloway [Scotland] having proved with a child, laid the same to a respectable man of the name John Woods, and persisted in his denial saying that he would never acknowledge the child unless his name was written at full length on its face; and he accordingly gave his solemn oath before the court to that effect. This made so much impression on the mind of the young woman, who was present, that his name and person remained constantly in her mind's eye, and when the child was born, the name of the father appeared in legible letters in the child's eye, the name of "JOHN WOODS", on the right eye, and 'BORN 1817" on the left eye. When John woods, the alleged father, came to know this circumstance, he instantly absconded and has not since been heard of. This wonderful child has now arrived in this city [Edinburgh] and has been inspected by the Professors and other learned Faculties of this city, and pronounced to be a most

wonderful phenomenon of nature, and an astonishing dispensation of Providence in pointing out the truth against the wicked and perjured ways of men."
(*T.E.C. Jr. M.D* 1976)

Ace of Spades in the Eye

A pregnant woman was engaged in a card party, and only wanted the ace of spades to win all that was staked and, as it happened, in the change of cards, the so such an effect upon her imagination that the child she was expecting at the time, when born, had the ace of spades depicted in the eye, and without injury to the organ of sight.

(*Johann Caspar Lavater*, 1804).

The 'Napoleon Eyed' Child

Countess de Boigne, in her interesting 'Memoires', relates that she once saw a little girl, *Josephine Louis,* born in 1824, with the words "*Napoleon Empereur*" in little letters on the iris around the pupils of her eyes.

The mother told the Countess how, while she was pregnant, she had lost and recovered a twenty-*sols* (shillings) coin. She was very fond of this coin because it was a parting gift from a beloved brother who had gone into the army; the coin was the model for the letters imprinted in the child's eyes.

An anecdote titled *'THE 'NAPOLEON' CHILD'* appeared in the *Mirror*, and is reproduced below:

"On Friday the 8th inst. [1828], we paid a visit to the Bazaar in Oxford Street, to witness this extraordinary sport of Nature, about which the French and English newspapers have lately been so communicative.

The child is an engaging little girl, about three years old. The colour of her eyes is pale blue, and on the iris, or circle round their pupils, the inscriptions on

Left eye	Right eye
NAPOLEON	EMPEREUR
EMPEREUR	NAPOLEO

may be traced in the above sized letters, although all the letters are not equally visible, the commencement "NAP" and "EMP" being the most distinct. The colour of the letters is almost white, and at first sight of the child they appear like rays, which make the eyes appear vivacious and sparkling. The accuracy of the inscriptions is much assisted by the stillness of the eye, on its being directed upwards, as to an object on the ceiling of the room & c; and with this aid the several letters may be traced with the naked eye.

This effect is accounted for by the child's mother earnestly looking at a franc-piece of Napoleon's, which was given to her by her brother previous to a long absence; and this operating during her pregnancy, has produced the appearance in question. It was visible at the child's birth, and has increased with her growth. She has been seen by Sir Astley Cooper and other leading members of the profession, and probably before our Number is published, she will have been shown to the King." (*Reuben Percy*, 1828).

The 'Elohim Eyed Boy'

In April 1701, John Evelyn, the famous English diarist, recorded the following phenomenon which he had observed at a fair in London:

"A Dutch boy of about eight or nine years old was carried about by his parents to show, who had about the iris of one eye, the letters of *DEUS MEUS*, and of the other *ELOHIM* in the Hebrew character. How this was done by artifice none could imagine; the parents affirming that he was so born. It did not prejudice his sight, and

he seemed to be a lively playing boy. Everybody went to see him; physicians and philosophers examined it with great accuracy, some considered it as artificial, others as almost supernatural."
(*Evelyn*, 1906).

Deus Meus translates into "My God" and *Elohim* is the Hebrew name for God.

Verses from the Quran on an Infant's Body

In 2009, in Dagestan, a small Russian village, text in Arabic from religious book started appearing on a nine-month-old child Ali Yakubov's back, arms, legs and stomach. Ali's parents were left stunned when the word *'Allah'* appeared on Ali Yakubov's chin soon after his birth. Since then, scores of writings in the Arabic script have appeared almost all over his body. Doctors say the markings are a medical mystery, but deny the possibilities of someone writing on the child's skin. *The Telegraph* reported pinkish in color and several centimeters high, the Quranic verse *"Be grateful to Allah"* was printed on the infant's right leg in clearly legible Arabic script.

There is an enormous body of evidence for this kind of occurrence of unusual images or letters in the eye, skin and other parts of the body.

Mike Foster of *Weekly World News* (21, November 2000) reports of an infant born with the spitting image of Jesus in its chest. Shawn Gelfand, son of Karen Gelfond, was born with a birthmark that looked uncannily like the face of Jesus Christ. The doctors who have examined the child have confirmed that the bizarre marking is indeed a genuine skin anomaly, not a tattoo or anything else fabricated by human hands.

In an article in the *International Journal of Parapsychology*, Professor Chari refers to the case of a female infant who was born with the curious birthmarks of the 'bangles' and 'necklaces' of the Hindu goddess *Kali*.

Reproduction of Target Images on Skin

Olga Kahl, a Russian-born clairvoyant living in Paris during the 1920s, provided some of the most impressive evidence of the representation of mental images in one person by bodily changes in another. On one occasion she misplaced a string of pearls; the loss pre-occupied her, and while the pearls were missing, she developed round areas of redness on the skin of her arms which suggested the form of the missing pearls. On another occasion, when living in Istanbul, she watched a group of dervishes, one of whom pushed a skewer through his cheek; the next day she developed an abscess of the cheek at the corresponding site where the dervish had pushed the skewer through.

Olga Kahl's experimental routine provided for a visitor or experimenter to write (hidden from her) a name or perhaps a design on a small piece of paper. The visitor rolled the piece of paper into a ball, which he kept in his hand without showing it to Olga Kahl. After a short interval, the name or design would appear on the skin of Olga Kahl's arm (sometimes on her upper chest). The letters would stand out in red, evidently from extremely localized changes in the superficial blood vessels. Sometimes a letter of a name was omitted, but then a space would be left for it, as if at some level Olga Kahl was aware of the entire word. Olga Kahl sometimes facilitated the process of her kind of dermographism by rubbing the part of her body where the letters were to appear; but such rubbing covered the entire area affected, and no one ever observed Olga Kahl in any endeavour to scratch the words on her skin.

Ian Stevenson, former head of the Department of Psychiatry at the University of Virginia, and a pioneer in reincarnation research, asserts that the mental image in the mind of the experimenter (who wrote the word or design on a piece of paper) had not directly influenced Olga Kahl's skin, and perhaps her mind obtained a copy, so to speak, of the experimenter's mental image and reproduced that on her skin. For example, when the target was the name 'Rene', the letter "N" came out resembling an "H" as in the alphabet of Olga's native Russian. (*Stevenson*, 1997)

Another case is that of a little girl upon whose skin appeared the answer to the sum she was trying to do!

Claude de Tisserant, who in the year 1775 wrote a book *De Prodiggis*, relates the following:

"The wife of a member of the Parliament of Provence in a dream saw her husband beheaded, which also really took place at the same time at Paris. Awaking in a passion of terror at the cruel spectacle, she found her hand convulsively shut, so that she was unable to open it; and when it was with main force opened by her maids, there was found on the palm the perfect image of her husband, with his head cut off, and this bled like the wounds of the stigmatized." (*Of the Nightmare*, 1845)

A very similar instance of the 'bodily imprint of mental images' is related by one Von Meyer:

"Madame V., of N, saw one night, in a very lively dream, a person who offered her a white and a red rose, bidding her choose one of them. She chose the red. When she awoke she felt a vehement burning in one arm, and by degrees there formed itself on the spot so affected, the perfect picture of a red rose, which appeared embossed on the skin, like a mole. On the eighth day this rose was in its most perfect state, both as to drawing and colour; it became thenceforth daily paler, and less defined, and after fourteen days no trace of it remained. This well authenticated fact forms an important contribution to the history of the *stigmata*.' (*Of the Nightmare*, 1845)

As early as the 13th century, Jacobus de Voragine assigned of the causes of these phenomena to mind and body interactions, thus taking them out of the category of the supernatural. And Joseph

Ennemoser (1787-1854), a South Tyrolean physician said, in reference to all such cases, "these appearances are not artificially produced deceptions, nor yet are they to be explained by the mere physical circumstances of the body. To spirits, or to any immediate divine operation, we will hardly ascribe them. Far from being miraculous, it is in every case a purely physiological process, grounded in a psychic cause."

Bill Jay, in his '*Animal Knickknacks—odd items from the 19th century photographic press*', recounts the following fascinating incident.

"It seems that Mr. J. J. Davis of Findlay, Ohio, went out to feed his cow last year. When he left the house, he had a photograph in his pocket, but when he returned he discovered that it had disappeared. He made a long and anxious search for it, but could not find it. Recently the cow gave birth to a calf, and on the left side of the calf's neck was a hairless spot about six inches square. In the centre of the spot was a capital likeness of Mr. Davis, and that gentleman is of opinion that he must have dropped the photograph into the food that he gave the cow on the occasion above mentioned, and she had eaten it. In some way, known only to the mysterious laws of nature, the photograph made an impression on the unborn calf. A number of Mr. J. J. Davis's friends have seen the calf in question, and they all corroborate his story."

The Recreative Magazine, Volume 1, reprinted by Monroe and Francis in 1822, carried the following curious cases:

At a place called Buch, near Versailles, lives a woman, the iris of whose eyes is divided into twelve sections, forming an exact dial, the figures resembling those found on the small watches that are included in rings worn on the finger. She was born with this peculiarity, and yet has the perfect use of her sight. (*The Eyes-Long Sight-Squinting*, 1821).

Again, on 4th January 1725, there was born at Blois a child named Marthurin Voiret. He had in each eye, a dial-plate of a watch, accurately painted; the hours were easily distinguished in Roman characters. His mother declared that while pregnant of this child, she had an ardent desire to see a watch. (*The Eyes-Long Sight-Squinting*, 1821)

There was also a man, who had a pair of the most pious peepers ever known: for in his eyes were these words distinct and legible, *sit nomen Domine benedictum* (a Latin phrase which means, 'Blessed in the name of the Lord'). Delafand is our authority for this account of one who not only had the fear of God before his eyes, but in his eyes!

The above cases, were they not clearly explainable on scientific grounds would almost appear to be incredible; but they are not even one-half so difficult to believe as that alleged marvelous discovery by Dr. Conyers who, it is said, on anatomizing a gentleman who died for love, found an impression of the lady's face upon his heart!

Professor H. Bernheim, in his famous work '*Suggestive Therapeutics*' states that he has been able to produce a blister on the back of a patient by applying a postage-stamp and suggesting to the patient that it was a fly-plaster. On this subject, Bernheim makes the following observation: "Finally, hemorrhages and bloody stigmata may be induced in certain subjects by means of suggestion."

MM. Bourru and Burot of Rochefort have experimented on the subject with a young marine, a case of hysteron-epilepsy. Dr. M. Bourru put a subject into the somnambulistic condition and gave him the following suggestion: "At four o'clock this afternoon, after the hypnosis, you will come into my office, sit down in the armchair, cross your arms upon your breast, and your nose will begin to bleed." At the hour appointed the young man did as directed. Several drops of blood came from the left nostril.

On another occasion, the same investigator traced the patient's name on both his forearms with the dull point of an instrument.

Then, when the patient was in the somnambulistic condition, he said, "At four o'clock this afternoon, you will go to sleep, and your arms will bleed along the lines which I have traced, and your name will appear written on your arms in letters of blood". He was watched at four o'clock and seen to fall asleep. On the left-arm the letters stood out in bright relief and in several places there were drops of blood. The letters were still visible three months afterwards, although they had gradually grown faint." (*Hudson*, 1892).

These instances *per se* make it clear that the human body is susceptible to the imprint of photograph—like images on it. If one understands and believes in this phenomenon of nature, then the intriguing question would arise—how are the exact images transferred to the skin or body? Who carries the information between hundreds of feet of distance? How does the human skin become susceptible to such impressions? These questions are so complicated that they cannot be answered in a single word or line. This phenomenon of pictorial impressions is related to various factors under various circumstances; but the underlying science should be the same for all cases. To simplify the matter, let's consider the following.

Atom is the smallest form of life and it is the building blocks that make up the Universe. Atoms are of course wave and particle in nature. Thus, all the objects we perceive and touch are fundamentally *'waves in nature'*. The forms and colour the objects hold are all wave-information which can be transferred from one place to another under appropriate circumstances. In other words, the Universe and the human body act as 'holograms'! This will be discussed in some more detail in the next chapter.

6

HOLOGRAPHIC BODY AND UNIVERSE

We human beings consider ourselves to be made up of "solid matter." Actually, the physical body is the end product, so to speak, of the subtle information fields, which mold our physical body as well as all physical matter. These fields are holograms which change in time (and are) outside the reach of our normal senses.

—Itzhak Bentov

P hysicists have discovered that all things in the universe are constantly vibrating, though at different frequencies. These vibrations generate wave fields that radiate from that objects that produce them. When the wave-field emanating from one object encounters another object, a part of it is reflected from the object that emitted the initial wave-field. The interference of the initial and the response wave-fields creates an overall pattern, and this pattern is effectively '*a hologram.*' It carries information on the objects that created the wave-fields.

Thus, it would be impossible to explain the organization of plants and animals solely in terms of physical and chemical forces. The shape of the body is a resemblance or an external manifestation of the 'holographic form.' Matter has no definite form or shape of its own. As the liquid or gas assumes the shape of their container, the material or physical body assumes the shape of the spiritual body. According to Plato in the Phaedrus (250 c), we are imprisoned in the body like an oyster in its shell.

It is known that when the antennae of a snail, the chelae of a crab, the feet of a salamander, or the head of a worm are amputated, these organs are regenerated even when the amputation is performed during their adult life. Spallanzani cut the feet and tail off the salamander six successive times and Bonnet seven times, and each time feet were reproduced of exactly the same size as the former ones without any increase or decrease in any part. These facts unambiguously demonstrate that the formative cause, whatever it may be, is always external to the part formed and that it exercises upon the whole development of that part and it remains intact even after completion of its works to get itself revived when nature so warrants. There must be some sort of pre-existing substratum, as upon a model, to guide the atoms and molecules during the entire process of regeneration, and each cell should be well aware of the blueprint—whole within the parts (a *substratum-superstratum* relationship).

The idea that there is a subtle body to guide the construction of human body is a popular subject of metaphysical and philosophical deliberations. Modern science has demonstrated that the human body—at the quantum level of information and energy—displays holographic properties. Each part of the body molecule or cell may encode information for the whole body. This fact has been successfully proven by various experiments in cloning by reconstructing the whole body from a single cell. These subtle holographic energy fields or patterns are the templates or blueprints for the physical body to guide its growth and development.

This is the principle underlying the doctrine of 'Cosmic Intelligence'. The Law of Correspondence states that what is true in the macrocosm (big universe) is also true in the microcosm (small universe, implying human body). *As is above, so is below*. Man is called a 'microcosm' (little universe) from his resembling the macrocosm (universe). In Indian *vedantic* philosophy, individual self is referred to as *'atman'* and cosmic self as *'Brahman'*.

Contemporary physicists are gradually realising the truths behind the ancient *vedantic* concepts of matter and energy. The need of the hour is to have these ancient concepts re-told in the language of the scientists. As back as 1844, chemist Liebig argued that in living bodies there is added a fourth cause which dominates the force of cohesion. Hans Driesh, the 19th century biologist, thought of this 'fourth cause' as the trans-temporal factor behind all organisms. Harold Saxton Burr, Ph.D., a Professor of Anatomy at the Yale University School of Medicine, steadfastly believed that life not only exhibited electromagnetic properties, but that these same properties were 'the organizing principle' that keep living tissue from falling into a chaotic state.

In recent times, Dr. Edgar Mitchell (former US astronaut and scientist), said that we, and ***every physical object***, have a resonant holographic image associated with our physical existence. It is called a Quantum Hologram (QH). To quote Dr. Mitchell:

". . . recognition that the quantum hologram is a macro-scale, non-local, information structure described by the standard formalism of quantum mechanism extends quantum mechanics to all physical objects including DNA molecules, organic cells, organs, brains and bodies. A laser hologram exhibits the distributive property. This means that a small part of a holographic record (for example, a hologram recorded on photographic film) contains the entire record of the recorded image, but with less visual brightness when reconstructed optically. Quantum holography appears to operate similarly in that emissions from complex matter, for example, biomatter, carry information about the entire organism. The fact that living cells in any organism evolve and grow from more simple cells, under the guidance of DNA molecules, implies quantum entanglement throughout the organism and its composite parts, with an associated instantaneous exchange of information through adaptive resonance. Thus some information about the entire organism is carried in the quantum emissions from its parts." (*Mitchell E.*, 2004)

How is the quantum hologram related to biological functions? Already, quantum physicists Fritz London and Niels Bohr had suggested that quantum phenomena might be essential for life processes. Recently, a wealth of evidence has demonstrated the importance of quantum mechanics for biological systems and thus a new field of quantum biology is emerging. (E. Mitchell, *Quantum Holography: A Basis for the Interface Between Mind and Matter,* 2004). John Eccles, who won a Noble prize in 1963 for his pioneering research on the synapse in the brain, suggested that a non-physical self enters our physical brain during embryological development and it might also survive the death of our physical body and brain.

Back in 1973, R. Miller and Webb suggested bioholograms as the projectors of our material reality. Miller and colleagues found that photons were being transmitted into radio waves through the genome.

"We think that these wave fronts interact with, interpenetrate with, and inter-determine the physical substance that makes up the creature. According to the holographic model of reality, all the objects we can observe are three-dimensional images formed of standing and moving waves by electromagnetic and nuclear processes . . . i.e., holograms. Just like a hologram encodes a 3D image, the Biohologram encodes and projects the blueprint of the human being, as well as other biological systems."
(Gariaev, et al, 2001; Miller, Miller and Webb, 2002)

Erwin Laszlo, the famous Hungarian scientist, assumes quantum vacuum as a universal field that interact with matter. He asserts that the field ". . . acts as a holographic medium, registering and conserving the scalar wave—transform of the 3-dimensional configuration spaces assumed by matter in space. This universal fifth field is not inferred from space-time interactions like gravitational, electromagnetic, the strong and weak nuclear forces. In this new type of field, space and time become implicate, enfolded, as described mathematically by Bohm. The fifth field is spectrally (holographically) organized, and is made of the energy present in the interference patterns of the waveforms. The transformations from space-time order to this spectrum dimension are described by holographic mathematical formulations."

Laszlo further asserts that fields can account for a variety of generative and regenerative processes in biology; it is likely to become a central notion in post-Darwinian theory. Current evidence points to a radiation field acting on matter in general and on living organisms in particular. The system settles into a new configuration, called the "super radiant vacuum", where most of the components are kept in phase by a time-oscillating electromagnetic field that is constant over a coherence domain.

In 1980, a Chinese named Zhang Yingquing published an extraordinary paper entitled, '*The Hologrammatic Rule of Living Beings*', treating the matter in detail. He writes:

"Each part of the hologram that is a living being has a corresponding position in the whole, or in another hologram. Each part of a hologram, plus its corresponding locus in the whole, or a non-corresponding locus in another hologram, is of a size comparable to the biological entity in the corresponding position. The laws of distribution of each part in a hologram are the same as those in each corresponding part of a whole, or of another hologram. Each hologram contained the special biological information proper to each part of a whole, as well as each point in another hologram. This is similar to the way in which each fragment of a hologrammatic photo contains the information for the whole picture."
(*Chen Kaiguo*, 1998).

Many extant literatures on 'near-death-experiences' strongly suggest that the human personality exists as both a physical body and a spiritual body.

Barbara Brennan, former research scientist for NASA, has been studying the 'human energy fields' for more than twenty years. She says 'human energy field' has an organising effect on matter and builds forms. These invisible fields form the templates for the formation of the bio-molecular body. Brennan, through her 'higher sense perception', observes that an 'energy field matrix' in the shape of a leaf is projected by a plant prior to the growth of a leaf, and then the leaf grows into that already existing form. In other words, the subtle energy fields act as a template for the growth of the visible material leaf.

Dr. Leonard Ravitz at William & Mary University says that the invisible electric fields serve as an electronic matrix to keep the corporeal form in shape.

Metaphysicist Annie Besant reported as early as in 1904 that during human antenatal life a single thread weaves a network, a shimmering web of inconceivable fineness and delicate beauty with minute meshes. Within the meshes of this web the coarser particles of the bodies are built together.

The list of ideas concerning human energy interference patterns and their connection with quantum holography could be continued for long, but it is not our task here.

All these evidences leave us little escape from the conclusion that the bio-matter of organisms—atoms, cells, molecules or tissues, contains the entire blueprint of the organism. This subtle 3-d body is a bio-hologram which carries the entire geometric information of the body it constitutes. This information can be carried to any distance by any wave-form of coherent type.

The electromagnetic waves produced by lightning are coherent waves capable of carrying with them the holographic geometric information of objects they pass through. At this junction, a question may arise—how the exact visual information is transmitted without any medium? Here comes the Fourier Transformations.

These holographic transformations form space-time order from a spectral dimension of frequencies. The mathematical formulation forming the basis of the holographic transformation is called 'Fourier Transformations' after the 18th century French mathematician who described it. Gabor applied Fourier Transformations to the creation of the hologram showing how Fourier Transformations of the interference pattern can be used to rebuild the virtual image of the object by the application of the inverse process. He demonstrated that from a dimension of frequencies, objects in space-time can be rebuilt in a virtual form.

A Fourier Transform (FT) is a mathematical way of expressing or transforming any simple or complex pattern (for instance, a picture or image or a design) into a language of simple waves and these waveforms can again be transformed into the respective patterns or images.

Mathematically speaking, an FT converts a function of time [f (t)] into a function of frequency [f (jw)] where j indicates that it is a complex function of frequency. In other works, FT can covert a signal from the time-domain to the frequency-domain. A Fourier Transform could also be used to covert something from a spatial location-domain (the coordinates in space) to a frequency-domain. The Fourier Transform looks like a random pattern of light, but it actually contains information of spatial and angular distribution of light in the image. In the mathematics of information theory, it is the Fourier Transform that is the workhouse providing the connection between the time domain and the frequency domain.

Place an image (for example, a slide transparency) at the focal length of the lens, and illuminate that slide with coherent light. At the other focus of the lens is placed a frosted glass screen. In this case, the lens will automatically perform a Fourier Transform on the input image, and project it onto the frosted glass screen. For example, if the input image is a sinusoidal grating, as show below, the resultant Fourier image will have a bright spot at the centre, with two flanking peaks on either side, whose distance from the centre will vary with the spatial frequency of the sinusoid.

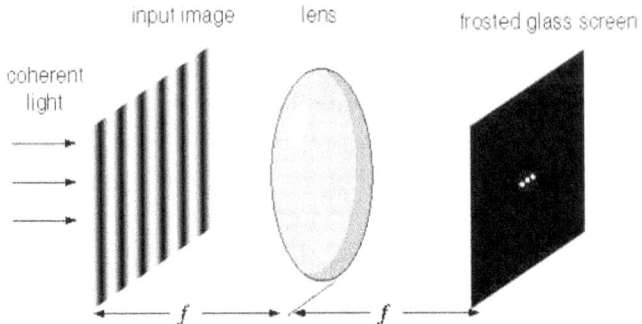

We can now see the mechanism underlying transfer of images. Every point on the input image radiates an expanding cone of rays towards the lens, but since the image is at the focus of lens, those rays will be reflected into a parallel beam that illuminates the entire image at the ground-glass screen. In other words, every point of the input image is spread uniformly over the Fourier image, where constructive and destructive interference will automatically produce proper Fourier representation.

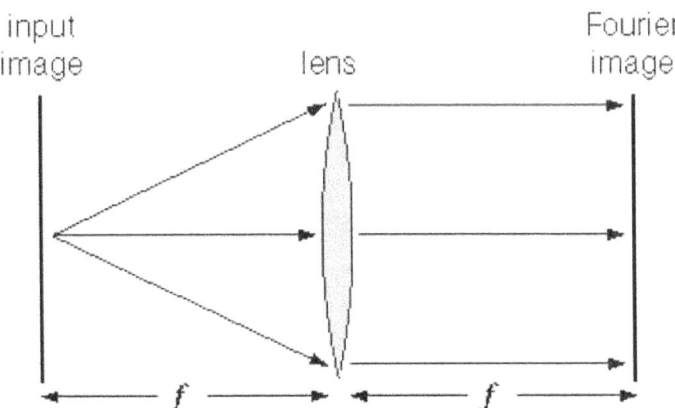

Conversely, parallel rays from the entire input image are focused onto the single central point of the Fourier image, where it defines the Central DC term by the average brightness of the input image.

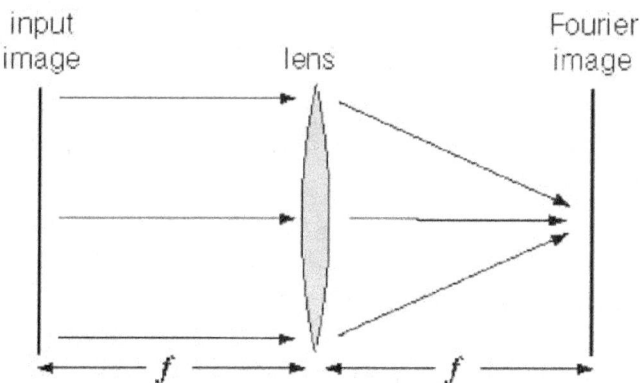

Note that the optical Fourier transform automatically operates in the reverse direction also, where it performs an inverse Fourier transform, converting the Fourier representation back into a spatial brightness image. Mathematically, the forward and inverse transforms are identical except for a minus sign that reverses the direction of the computation.

After years of research, French Baron Jean-Baptiste-Joseph Fourier discovered this powerful tool in the early 1800s, naming it the 'Fourier Transform'.

Norbert Wiener, who pioneered the word 'cybernetics' in his book of the same name published in 1946, used the mathematics of Fourier to analyze and to model the activity of brain waves in both the time domain (Td) and the frequency domain (Fd). Yale Professor Dr. Ronald Coifman holds the FT as 'nature's way of analyzing data' and describes that to form an image on our retina, the lens in our cye performs Fourier Transformations on the light that enters it. The tool of Fourier Transform is truly ubiquitous in nature, as our eyes and ears have subconsciously performed the Fourier Transform to interpret sound and light waves. In the 1930s, Russian scientist Nikolai Berstein discovered that our physical movements might be encoded in our brains in a language of Fourier wave forms. Pribram proved that dedicated nerve cells in the eye respond to certain frequencies of electromagnetic waves that hit the eye. The picture is viewed as a set of frequencies and not as individual dots or pixels. Now how can a picture contain frequencies you may ask? Or, how can an image be represented as 'wave'? Well, as we know, spatial information can be translated into a frequency spectrum and back into the spatial domain by Fourier Transforms.

Parallax and Viewing at an Angle

Parallax and viewing at an angle are the consistent features of a hologram. While looking at the stereo-metric holographic displays, one can move one's head and can observe the continuous changing of the image aspect with the viewing angle. Another trait of a hologram is an optimal viewing distance to see the image.

In many of the cases of lightning imprints, this effect of parallax or 'viewing at an angle' has been evidently recorded by the observers. In the case of steam boat image recorded on an opposite mirror, the observer could notice it only when standing almost parallel with the mirror and not otherwise. Similarly, in the case of the Mexican marble which bore upon its face a beautiful mountain landscape, the picture was not visible under gas or electric light but it was vivid under the sun light. In some other cases, the images were noticeable only when the sun was in a certain position. The persons who noticed the mysterious faces appearing on window panes have also recorded that they were able to see the images plainly when standing at a certain angle with the panes. I.N. Brown, M.D., who observed as many as four faces in the window panes of the Nicholas Building removed the sash and brought them under a well-controlled lightning atmosphere. But the views of the images were not as satisfactory as in its natural place in the window.

Readers may also note that the clearness of the lightning figures is increased under the ambient conditions. For instance, in the case of the image resembling Jesus Christ appearing in the window of Jim Steven's truck, whenever there is morning dew, the image reappears and gets vanished in the day when the dew evaporates.

Similarly, the image of the 'Russellville Girl' re-appeared on every occasion when it rained. The image of Our Lady that appeared on a pane of glass in Absam, Austria disappears when the glass pane is immersed in water and re-appears when the glass dries.

There are other remarkable features of these lightning imprints which attest the optical effect of their cause. In some cases, especially where portraits of more than one person are displayed, the figures seem to overlap each other. In one extraordinarily case, the face of a woman was imprinted on the window pane in a very peculiar way. It was a whole face, which was formed of numerous small faces. Together, all these observations clearly suggest the 'holographic' nature of the lightning imprints.

It must be mentioned here that in these cases the images are of the same size as the originals; but in some of the cases cited by M. Poey, they must have been 'optical images' such as are produced in the *camera obscura*. The complete image of a young marple-tree on the body of a little girl must have been reduced; and we know of no natural mode of effecting such reduction except by optical means. But how, it may be asked, could be impression be made through the clothes of the victim?

M. Poey says, "The fact that impressions are made through garments is easily accounted for, when we remember that their rough texture does not prevent the lightning from passing through them with the impression it has received." To corroborate this view, he then mentions an instance of lightning passing down a chimney and entering a truck, in which was found an inch of soot, which must have passed through the wood itself.

In cases of lightning imprints of surrounding scenic beauty, one wonders what would have been the causes to condense the surroundings, whose dimensions are some twenty or thirty yards, into an image an inch long, imprinted on the skin. This is in fact a lens-like effect of hologram. Though the fidelity and exactness of the image information is regarded in its entirety, the geometric size may vary to accommodate the available space.

7

CONCLUSION

The observations that are not explained by current scientific theories are the most valuable, for they may propel the field forward in the next cycle of innovation, possibly to a paradigm shift.

—D.L. Jewett

Nature has an inherent tendency to transmit information in the form of *'pictorial representations.'* The extraordinary effects produced on the unborn child by the sudden mental emotions of the mother are remarkable examples of this kind on the sensitive surfaces of living forms. It is doubtless true that the mind's action in such cases may increase or diminish the molecular deposits in the several portions of the system. The precise place which each separate particle assumed in the new organic structure may be determined by the influence of thought or feeling. If in the mother exists any unusual tendency of the vital forces to the brain, at the critical period, there will be a similar cerebral development and activity in the child. Such transfer of mental pictures from the mother to her child is a quantum process i.e., transfer of information from a quantum holographic system to its subsystem. Needless to say, as a child is a subsystem in the mother-child matrix, so are the human beings to the universe as a system[5]. As the mental images sometimes get transferred to the child, the scenic beauty of adjacent objects is sometimes imprinted on the skin of the nearby people by the wonderful action of lightning. These phenomena of lightning imprints imply, among other things, that the information in the form of pictorial representations can be transferred onto the human skins without the aid of any intervening physical medium and that the human skin is susceptible to imprinting of such pictorial images.

Madame Blavatsky suggested that this spontaneous photography provides a way of understanding how mental images of the mother are transmitted to the body of the child. Her explanation depends upon the principle that a pregnant woman is not only 'highly impressive'; but also, so to speak, actively impressive. She writes:

"Her *pores* are opened; she exudes an *odic* emanation which is but another form of the *akasa*, the electricity, or life-principle, and which, according to Reichenbach, produces mesmeric sleep, and consequently is magnetism. Magnetic currents develop themselves into electricity upon their exit from the body. An object making a violent impression on the mother's mind, its image is instantly projected into the astral light, or the universal ether, which Jevons and Babbage, as well as the authors of the *Unseen Universe*, tell us is the repository of the spiritual images of all forms and even human thoughts. Her magnetic emanations attract and unite themselves with the descending current which already bears the image upon it. It rebounds, and repercussing more or less violently, impresses itself upon the foetus."

Blavatsky notes the relations between maternal impressions and the mimicry of the crucifixion involved in the stigmata, and records a story (from Catherine Crowe's well-known *Night-Side of*

---

[5] The author is working on this aspect of research. Readers may be pleased to read his next book "Inherited Impressions: Some Curious Effects of Holographic Mind Process" which will be in the press soon.

Nature) of the traumatic doubling of skin-impressions. The story goes on that two young ladies in Poland, were standing by an open window during a storm; a flash of lightning fell near them, and the gold necklace on the neck of one of them was melted. A perfect image of it was impressed upon the skin, and remained throughout life. The other girl, appalled by the accident to her companion, stood transfixed with horror for several minutes, and then fainted away. Little by little, the same mask of a necklace as had been instantaneously imprinted upon her friend's body, appeared upon her own, and remained there for several years, when it gradually disappeared.

Unfortunately, many ancient concepts and ideas are totally eclipsed as quaint eccentricity and nonsensical based on myths and fables. It is true, not because of insufficient evidence, but rather for want of theoretical construct which could place it within the prevailing paradigms of science. There are hundreds of natural phenomena that escaped proper scientific investigation and inquiry. One such natural phenomenon is the photographic effect of lightning. It is not a crude idea based upon a theory spurted out of fertile imagination. It has its origin in the observation of nature's own process. True, there were in the past many tales conjured up by the magic want of fancy which dazzled for a time. Many such fanciful theories have rightly been rejected as worthless. But casting doubts upon every other assertion, like the one relating to lightning photography, is unwise.

As we have seen so far, the evidences for 'lightning photographs' is overwhelming. This 'mysterious' effect has been well documented but has not been studied and examined properly. The only escape from such a conclusion is a willingness to overlook the most competent evidences of the fact. Should the non-tree-like images produced by the lightning be ignored, this wonderful phenomenon of nature will forever escape scientific scrutiny and explanation.

We cannot scorn these evidences just because they were made mostly by personal observations, many of which were made by laymen. They had the chance to see them and accidently come across such wonderful imprints of nature. They wanted to spread the knowledge about them so that everybody may know of it. Therefore, they have recorded the instances of lightning photographs to their best. It is for the scientists to make a proper investigation of the facts and ascertain their credentials. The question of the truth is left to their decision. Our conclusions are limited to that the available evidences ought to be examined and if found true, the world may have the benefit of knowledge.

Here a question may arise as to why the lightning imprints in most of the cases relate to religious imagery like crosses, crucifix, Virgin Mary, Jesus Christ etc. What law governs such resemblance? The answer is simple. Religion-related imagery attracts the attention of the public easily and gets published widely.

An instance is the sudden appearance of the Virgin Mary's image on a window pane in a Malaysian hospital. This incident made the Catholics excited who flocked to the hospital to pray, worship and freak out after seeing the image. The news spread like wildfire among the local Christians on Facebook.

If the imprint of the Virgin Mary's image on the window pane is a work of lightning, then such a phenomenon cannot be experimented within the four rooms of a scientific laboratory. Nature itself teaches us—like the fall of apple enlightened Newton. What is expected of us is simple. Pay a little attention. How could an image resembling the Virgin Mary get imprinted on a window pane located in the seventh floor of a hospital? It is an artifact or natural? If natural, what could have been the factors? Does the image have any similarity to the statue of the Virgin Mary situated near the hospital? These are the questions the academic experts should attempt to answer without leaving the responsibility to the observers.

It is time, however that this extraordinary effect of lightning should be viewed in a perfectly different light, because, if the conclusions I have drawn are correct, they will throw considerable light on Nature's code, and the entire scheme of the Universe. We have to regard this extraordinary phenomenon as a new field of research opened to investigation by modern scientists who have to lay the foundation of a new branch of science—*keraunography*, in the real sense of the term.

～

BIBLIOGRAPHY

(1839). *The Family magazine, 4*. J. A. James & Co.

(1884, October 17). *The Amateur Photographer*, 19.

(1888). *The Chicago Medical Times*, 20.

(1904). *The American Amateur Photographer*, p. 442.

A Ghost Story. (1889, October 21). Retrieved February 10, 2013, from Paperpast—Southland Times: http://paperspast.natlib. govt.nz/cgi-bin/paperspast?a=d&d=ST18891021.2.22

A Human Camera—Mystery of a Picture. (1904, September 14). *The Advertiser*.

A petrifaction and natural Dageuerreotype on Stone. (1856). *Friends Intelligencer*, p. 605.

Abrams, A. (1912). *New Concepts in Diagnosis and Treatment*. San Francisco: Philopolis Press.

Alabama: A Guide to the Deep South. (1941). Alabama State Planning Committee.

Another Picture on a Window-Pane. (1883, October 14). Retrieved February 12, 2013, from *The New York Times*: http://query. nytimes.com/mem/archive-free/pdf?res=F50A1FF73F5C15738 DDDAD0994D8415B8384F0D3

Aurora Daily Express. (1895, April 30). Retrieved February 11, 2013, from Google News: http://news.google.com/newspapers? nid=2329&dat=18950430&id=008oAAAAIBAJ&sjid=igUGA AAAIBAJ&pg=2165,4915501

Behold the image of Blessed Virgin Mary seen in New jersy. (n.d.). Retrieved January 22, 2013, from Ebere Inyam's Blog: http:// ebereinyama.blogspot.in/2012_10_01_archive.html

Belfast Telegraph. (2012, August 9). Retrieved February 2, 2013, from Face of Jesus Christ appears on tree stump at Belfast cemetery: http://www.belfasttelegraph.co.uk/news/ local-national/northern-ireland/face-of-jesus-christ-appears-on-tree-stump-at-belfast-cemetery-16195735.html

Benford, M. (2000-2001). Empirical Evidence Supporting Macro-scale quantum holography in non-local effcts. *Journal of Theoretics, Vol.2.*

Britain), R. M. (1903). Lightning Photography. *Quarterly Journal of the Royal Meteorological Society*, 288.

(1816). Lightning. In J. Brown, *Encyclopaedia Perthensis:or, Universal Dictioary of the Arts, Sciences, Literature & c intended to supersede the use of other books of reference.*

Camille, F. (1905). *Thunder and Lightning.* London: Chatto & Windus.

Chen Kaiguo, Z. S. (1998). *Opening the Dragon Gate: The Making of a Modern Taoist Wizard.* Tokyo: Tuttle Publishing.

Chronicling America. (1897, October 6). Retrieved February 7, 2013, from The Saint Paul Globe: http://chroniclingamerica. loc.gov/lccn/sn90059523/1897-10-06/ed-1/seq-3/;words=lightn ing+PICTURED+LIGHTNING

Circles, R. R. (n.d.). Retrieved January 22, 2013, from UFO Digest: http://www.ufodigest.com/cropcircles.html

Curous Lightning Freak. (1908, September 12). Retrieved February 11, 2012, from Paperspast: http://paperspast.natlib.govt.nz/ cgi-bin/paperspast?a=d&d=PBH19080912.2.82.45

D.K.Wilgus. (1970). The Girl in the Window. *Western Folklore*, 251-256.

Evelyn, J. (1906). *The diary of John Evelyn, Volume 1.* Routledge.

Faces in the Window. (n.d.). Retrieved February 10, 2013, from Real Ghost Pictures: http://www.realghostpictures.info/tag/ ghost-face-in-the-window/

Fidler, W. P. (2003). *Augusta Evans Wilson, 1835-1909.* University of Alabama Press.

Fort, C. (1974). *The Complete Books of Charles Fort.* New York: Dover.

Fort, C. (2004). *Wild Talents.* Cosimo, Inc.

Fortworth Daily Gazette. (1887, October 30). Retrieved February 2, 2013, from Portal to Texas History: http://texashistory.unt. edu/ark:/67531/metapth85606/m1/11/zoom/

Francis, M. a. (1820). Remarkable Effect of Lightning. *Spirit of the English Magazines, 7.*

Gallipolis Journal. (1875, December 2). Retrieved February 12, 2013, from Chronicling America: http://chroniclingamerica.loc. gov/lccn/sn85038121/1875-12-02/ed-1/seq-1/

Ghotly Girl in the Window. (n.d.). Retrieved February 10, 2013, from Real Ghost Pictures: http://www.realghostpictures.info/ tag/ghost-face-in-the-window/

Google News. (1908, August 8). Retrieved February 2, 2013, from The Pittsburg Press: http://news.google.com/newspapers?nid=1 144&dat=19080808&id=OQsbAAAAIBAJ&sjid=zUgEAAAA IBAJ&pg=3657,1389094

Gousseva, Maria. (2006, April 1). *Lightnings can select and pursue their victims, legends say.* Retrieved January 9, 2013, from Pravda.ru: http://english.pravda.ru/science/mysteries/01-04-2006/78209-lightning-0/

How Products are Made. (n.d.). Retrieved July 8, 2010, from www. madehow.com: http://www.madehow.com/Volume-3/Hologram. html

Hudson, T. (1892). *Law of Psychic Phenomenon* (Vol. 1). London: G. P. putname's sons.

Instances of Photography by Lightning. *Western Electrician, 1,* 139.

Instances of Photography by Lightning. (1887). *Western Electrician, 1-2*, p. 139.

Instantaneous Photography by Lightning. (1886, September 1). *Stevens Point (Wisconsin) Journal.*

J.D.Bell. (1869). On Pictures taken by Lightning. *Appletons' journal: a magazine of general literature*, 302-303.

Jitatmananda, S. (1993). *Holistic Science and Vedanta.* Bombay: Bharatiya Vidya Bhavan.

Johann Caspar Lavater, T. H. (1804). *Essays on physiognomy: for the promotion of the knowledge and the love of mankind,.* H. D. Symonds.

John Holmes Agnew, W. H. (1862). Singular Phenomenon. *Eclectic magazine: foreign literature,* 287.

Kentucky News Era. (1913, November 20). Retrieved February 13, 2013, from Google News: http://news.google.com/newspapers ?nid=266&dat=19131120&id=z4NQAAAAIBAJ&sjid=QDQN AAAAIBAJ&pg=2972,4330025

Leith, J. U. (1964). Lenless Photography. *SPIE Photo-Optics Workshop Meeting: New Technologies for Data Recording and Display,* (pp. 8-14). Los Angeles, California.

Lightning as a Photographer. (1904, March 13). *The New York Times.*

Lightning strikes man in his mouth for smoking. (2005, June 5). Retrieved February 10, 2013, from http://english.pravda.ru/ society/stories/03-06-2005/8355-lightning-0/

(1902). In S. N. Lockyer, *Nature* (p. 158). New York: Macmillan Journals Ltd.

Marvellous Freaks of Lightning. (1916). *Otago Witness,* p. 35.

Mitchell. (1999/2002). *Nature's Mind: The Quantum Hologram.* available at http://www.edmitchellapollo14.com/naturearticle. htm.

Mitchell, E. (2004). Quantum Holography. In M. S. Paul J. Rosch, *Bioelectromagnetic medicine.* Informa Health Care.

Murray, J. (1833). *The description of a new lightning conductor ; and observations on the phenomena of the thunder storm.* S. Highley.

Of the Nightmare. (1845). *Dublin University Magazine: a literary and political journal,* 25.

Otago Witness. (1875, March 6). Retrieved February 28, 2013, from Papers Past: http://paperspast.natlib.govt.nz/ cgi-bin/paperspast?a=d&d=OW18750306.2.7&e=—10—1- byDA—0Santos+Brazil—

Our Lady of Absam. (n.d.). Retrieved January 22, 2013, from Holy Face of Manoppello: http://holyfaceofmanoppello.blogspot. in/2011/03/our-lady-of-absam.html

Our Views. (1884, October 17). *The Amateur Photographer,* 19.

Photograph by Lightning. (1923, November 9). *The Singapore Free Press and Mercantile Advertiser (1884-1942).*

Photographed by Lightning. (1892, July 23). *Western Electrician.*

Photographed by Nature. (1890, February 21). *The Anaconda standard,* p. 3.

Photography by Lightning. (1908, May 11). *Ashburton Guardian, xxix (7482),* 4.

R.Lipkin. (1996). Holograms Serve as guiding light for atoms. *Science News,* Vol 149, page 263.

Reuben Percy, J. T. (1828). *The Mirror of literature, amusement, and instruction,* p. 99.

Richard Alan Miller, B. W. (2007). Embryonic Holography. *DNA Monthly Magazine.*

Rickard, B. (n.d.). *Tattoos from the Blue.* Retrieved January 7, 2013, from Forteantimes: http://www.forteantimes.com/features/articles/3292/tattoos_from_the_blue.html

Russian Researchers claim to have solved Mystery of Crop Circles. (n.d.). Retrieved March 3, 2013, from ufodigest.com: http://www.ufodigest.com/cropcircles.html

Shrine of Our Lady of Absam. (n.d.). Retrieved January 22, 2013, from Sacred Destinations: http://www.sacred-destinations.com/austria/absam-shrine-of-our-lady

Shumaker, W. (1989). *Natural magic and modern science: four treatises, 1590-1657.* Center for Medieval and Early Renaissance Studies, State University of New York at Binghamton.

Slawinski, J. (1987). Electromagnetic Radiation and the Afterlife. *Journal of Near-Death Studies,* 79-94.

Society, R. M. (1903). Lightning Photography. *Quarterly Journal of the Royal Meteorological Society.*

Spence, L. (n.d.). Encyclopedia of Occultism and Parapsychology.

Splitter, H. W. (1955). Nature's Strange Photographs. *Fate Magazine.*

Stevenson, I. (1997). *Where reincarnation and biology intersect.* Praeger Publishers.

Strange Effect of Lightning. (1940, December 3). Retrieved February 15, 2013, from *The Sydney Morning Herald*: http://nla.gov.au/nla.news-article17706531

(1821). The Eyes-Long Sight-Squinting. In *The Recreative review, or Eccentricities of literature and life* (p. 178). London: Wallis & Co.

The Interior Journal. (1880, April 30). Retrieved February 7, 2013, from Chronicling America: http://chroniclingamerica. loc.gov/lccn/sn84038328/1880-04-30/ed-1/seq-4/;words=pane+lightning

The Miami News. (1953, January 26). Retrieved February 9, 2013

The Queer Photograph on the Wall. (1896, March 3). Retrieved February 8, 2013, from The New York Times: http://query. nytimes.com/mem/archive-free/pdf?res=F60C11FF3C5C17738 DDDAA0894DB405B8685F0D3

The Rice belt journal. (1907, November 29). Retrieved February 12, 2013, from Chronicling America: http://chroniclingamerica. loc.gov/lccn/sn88064402/1907-11-29/ed-1/seq-3/;words=perfe ct+photograph+flower+stood+which+mirror

The Saint Paul Globe. (1897, October 6). Retrieved February 7, 2013, from Chronicling America: http://chroniclingamerica.loc. gov/lccn/sn90059523/1897-10-06/ed-1/seq-3/;words=lightning +PICTURED+LIGHTNING

The St.Louis Republic. (1904, August 8). Retrieved February 9, 2013

Timbs, J. (1858). Photographic Effects of Lightning. In J. Timbs, *Curiosities of Science, Past and Present: A book for old and young.* Kent.

Times Daily. (1908, October 9). Retrieved February 12, 2013, from Google News: http://news.google.com/newspapers?nid=1842& dat=19081009&id=yQgsAAAAIBAJ&sjid=CMgEAAAAIBAJ &pg=659,1589297

Todd, R. B. (1839). Generation. *The cyclopaedia of anatomy and physiology, 2.*

Tomorrow. (1952). *Tomorrow*, 79.

Utah Journal. (1880, July 2). Retrieved February 20, 2013, from Utah State University Digital Collections: http://folkbistro. usu.edu/cdm/compoundobject/collection/utahj2/id/33123/ show/33176/rec/98

W. & R. Chambers. (1868). *Chambers's encyclopædia: a dictionary of universal knowledge.*

William Chambers, R. C. (1861). *Chamber's journal of popular literature, science and arts.* W & R Chambers.

Window cleared on the Sexton House; Lightning tale resurrected. (2009). Retrieved February 10, 2013, from Newsdemocratleader: http://newsdemocratleader.com/ bookmark/1631513-Window-cleared-on-the-Sexton-House-Lightning-tale-resurrected

INDEX

www.ingramcontent.com/pod-product-compliance
Lightning Source LLC
Chambersburg PA
CBHW070706290526
45790CB00001B/477